"But for a Small Moment"

Neal A. Maxwell

"But for a Small Moment"

BOOKCRAFT
Salt Lake City, Utah

Library of Congress Catalog Card Number: 85-73652
ISBN 0-88494-585-5

First Printing, 1986

Printed in the United States of America

Contents

Acknowledgments

In a work of this type, which involves considerable research and deals with much historical detail, I simply could not have attempted to cover the ground without the help of able scholars. Hugh Nibley stands out with his remarkable output of books and articles over the years. His torch, which burns brightly still, has lighted others in turn, some of whom have assisted with this work while of course remaining in no way accountable for its inadequacies.

I offer special appreciation to Truman Madsen, Dan Ludlow, Roy Doxey, and Elizabeth Haglund, who were kind enough to review the whole manuscript and to make excellent suggestions concerning its structure, emphases, and balance.

I express particular thanks also to others, such as S. Kent Brown for his help with chapters pertaining to our premortal existence, and to Richard Anderson for assistance on the historicity of Jesus in the secular area. Similarly Blake Ostler gave welcome help with the chapters on premortality, and Dean Jessee with the portions surrounding the events at Liberty Jail.

Additionally I give thanks to Grant Anderson, Richard Anderson, Jack Welch, and Robert Matthews for helpful suggestions made in connection with other projects of mine which have found their way into this manuscript.

I extend a special expression of gratitude to George Bickerstaff for his editorial watchcare. Observing him do his work has been a delight.

As always I express deep appreciation to Susan Jackson, who was so helpful in processing the various drafts which were necessary as this book took shape.

Finally, my thanks once again to my wife, who patiently gave up some July days and evenings with me so that this work could go forward.

This is not an official Church publication, and I alone am responsible for the views it expresses.

Key to Abbreviations

The following abbreviations have been used to simplify references in the text of this work:

Bushman	Richard L. Bushman. *Joseph Smith and the Beginnings of Mormonism*. Chicago: University of Illinois Press, 1984.
BYU Studies	*Brigham Young University Studies*. Provo, Utah: Brigham Young University Press. Published quarterly.
Comprehensive History	B. H. Roberts. *A Comprehensive History of The Church of Jesus Christ of Latter-day Saints*. 6 vols. Salt Lake City: Deseret News Press, 1930.
Discourses of Brigham Young	Brigham Young. *Discourses of Brigham Young*. Selected by John A. Widtsoe. Salt Lake City: Deseret Book Co., 1941.
Doctrines of Salvation	Joseph Fielding Smith. *Doctrines of Salvation*. Compiled by Bruce R. McConkie. 3 vols. Salt Lake City: Bookcraft, 1954–56.
Gospel Doctrine	Joseph F. Smith. *Gospel Doctrine*. Salt Lake City: Deseret Book Co., 1939.
History of the Church	Joseph Smith. *History of The Church of Jesus Christ of Latter-day Saints*. 7 vols. Salt Lake City: Deseret Book Co., 1927 (published by the Church).
Journal of Discourses	*Journal of Discourses*. 26 vols. Liverpool: F. D. and S. W. Richards, 1854.

A Plainer Translation	Robert J. Matthews. *"A Plainer Translation": Joseph Smith's Translation of the Bible, A History and Commentary.* Provo: Brigham Young University Press, 1975.
The Restoration of Plain and Precious Things	Monte S. Nyman and Robert L. Millet, eds. *The Joseph Smith Translation: The Restoration of Plain and Precious Things.* BYU Religious Studies Center, 1985.
Teachings	Joseph Smith. *Teachings of the Prophet Joseph Smith.* Compiled by Joseph Fielding Smith. Salt Lake City: Deseret Book Co., 1976.
Timely and Timeless	Hugh W. Nibley. *Nibley on the Timely and the Timeless: Classic Essays of Hugh W. Nibley.* BYU Religious Studies Center, 1978.
Words	Andrew F. Ehat and Lyndon W. Cook, eds. *The Words of Joseph Smith.* BYU Religious Studies Center, 1980.
Writings	Joseph Smith. *The Personal Writings of Joseph Smith.* Compiled and edited by Dean Jessee. Salt Lake City: Deseret Book Co., 1984.

Introduction

Artist[1] Al Rounds's painting which graces the cover of this book is a reminder of a very difficult but also a very productive and significant period in the ministry of the Prophet Joseph Smith.

The lonely, limestone Missouri jailhouse (twenty by twenty-two feet) was more a dungeon than a cell. Ironically, because of its location in that city it was known as the Liberty Jail.[2] Herein, during his incarceration (December 1, 1838, through April 6, 1839) as a result of betrayals and distortions by some "friends" as well as enemies, the Prophet Joseph Smith received some of the most rich and remarkable revelations ever given to any prophet. The double walls, four feet thick, kept Joseph and his companions in, but they could not keep the Spirit and revelation out. Though Joseph's physical vision suffered from incessant gloom, the "choice seer" had that vision which mattered most.

Because of its spiritual significance, Elder B. H. Roberts called this forbidding place the "prison-Temple." (*Comprehensive History*, 1:521.)

The nearly windowless prison-temple becomes a unique window itself through which to view Joseph and the processes of revelation and soul stretching evident during this particular period of the Restoration. Herein we see Joseph testifying while suffering, learning while teaching, giving direction to the work while he was being tutored, giving blessings while being cursed, and proclaiming the United States Constitution to be "a glorious standard" even while being grossly deprived of his own constitutional rights.

The scene, therefore, is not one of an isolated prophet insulated in a calm, scholastic or monastic setting. Rather we see a prophet removed from but still very much involved in the fray. Though Joseph had been betrayed, jailed, and defamed, the Lord's work went on through him in the midst of "all these things."

For Joseph it was a time not only for receiving additional revelation but also for contemplating what he had already received. Hence the relevance of chapters 2 through 5 of this work. Moreover, throughout this volume the interplay of various scriptures, revelations, and blessings will be shown. All demonstrate evidence of God's guiding and correlating hand.

Significantly, through the "window" that was Liberty Jail we see Joseph growing spiritually and being prepared for the rushed moments in another and final jail—Carthage.[3]

In Liberty, Joseph had time to ponder, albeit in grim conditions. Jailed Joseph's introspections doubtless prepared him to receive therein the great revelations now known as sections 121 and 122 of the Doctrine and Covenants. Section 123 was set forth by Joseph during the same period of incarceration. Portions of these revelations and Joseph's own communications and reflections during his imprisonment illuminate for us, in ways probably unique in all of scripture, the challenges associated with deepening one's discipleship.

We might note too that, while the Prophet's time in the prison-temple separated him physically from his people, it also yielded a recognition of his need to improve communications with Church members. He noted with resolve that the devil had hampered and distressed him "from the beginning to keep me from explaining myself to them and I never have had opportunity to give them the plan that God has revealed to me" (*Writings,* p. 387). After the Missouri incarceration Joseph appeared to be more assertive and directive and declarative than before, to be even more of a shepherd and a spokesman. Though he was told in jail that "thy years shall not be numbered less" (D&C 122:9), Joseph nevertheless knew that he did not have an abundance of years left to him.

If at this and at other times in the Prophet's life one sees in a developing Joseph some impulsiveness in support of a transcendent cause, this merely tends to bring to mind the instance of anxious and protective Peter's cutting off the ear of the high priest's servant (John 18:10, 26).

If Joseph had a contempt for certain civil, political, and military leaders who abused and vexed him, one recalls too how Peter and others also at the direction of civil and religious authorities were unjustly reproved, beaten, and commanded not to speak again of Jesus, but who, when freed, likewise promptly resumed their ministries and "ceased not to teach and preach Jesus Christ" (Acts 5:40–42).

If the Prophet Joseph had stern words for his persecutors and spoke of the apostate conditions which necessitated his heavenly call, he was also like another martyr, Stephen. Both men saw "two beings," Jesus being "on the right hand of God," and both were slain for their reproving testimonies (see Acts 7:51–60). In fact, the experiences in the prison-temple only underscored, for Joseph, his colleagueship with earlier prophets and martyrs.

In all of this, as Elder B. H. Roberts wrote, Joseph, at times, "loosened the flood tide of his over-wrought emotions, and in them the greatness of his soul is often revealed" (*Comprehensive History*, 1:523). Today's Church members are used to seeing as prophets older men who are well established and experienced by many years of high leadership positions. Liberty Jail featured a thirty-three-year-old Prophet whose expressions about his frustrations reflected his years. The soul stretching was not accomplished without pain and the signs of such pain.

The window that is Liberty Jail frames a great teaching episode as if it were frozen in time and space for us to see and to study. But this window is not only for pondering the past: it is a window also for derivatively and instructively viewing oneself and the Church. Those who so do will encounter abundant lessons for today and tomorrow.

At several times in the brief history of The Church of Jesus Christ of Latter-day Saints, its enemies probably felt that it had been successfully disposed of; and superficial indicators encouraged such a mistaken view. Clearly, one such time occurred in the 1838–1839 period in Missouri. Twelve thousand Church members were then driven from Missouri to an area centering on Quincy, Illinois. A few were slain,[4] and their Prophet was jailed.

Nevertheless, from the prison-temple Joseph the seer wrote, "Zion shall yet live though she seemeth to be dead" (*Writings,* p. 382). Joseph's trust in God's unfolding purposes in the midst of such adversity was grounded on revelation concerning the plan of salvation and the unique doctrine of the premortal existence of man. Hence chapters 4 and 5 of this work.

It was precisely during this express time of peril that the Lord spoke reassuring and informing words to the imprisoned Joseph Smith concerning the rolling on of the latter-day work and promised a continued flow of revealed knowledge: "How long can rolling waters remain impure? What power shall stay the heavens? As well might man stretch forth his puny arm to stop the Missouri river in its decreed course, or to turn it up stream, as to hinder the Almighty from pouring down knowledge from heaven upon the heads of the Latter-day Saints." (D&C 121:33.)

The mighty Missouri could not, in fact, be turned upstream. Neither would the Lord's work be altered from its "decreed course," just as the words Joseph translated ten years earlier assured: "For the eternal purposes of the Lord shall roll on, until all his promises shall be fulfilled" (Mormon 8:22).

In Moses' day the Lord let his doctrine "drop as the rain" (Deuteronomy 32:2). In Eli's day "there was no open vision," and the paucity of revelation caused the "word of the Lord" to be "precious" (1 Samuel 3:1). In Joseph Smith's time, heavenly knowledge would be "poured" upon the heads of the Latter-day Saints in a cascade of "plain and precious" truths. The persecution in Missouri thus not only failed to destroy the kingdom; it induced further revelation and determination, which was followed by further consolidation in Nauvoo, which in turn was followed by the establishment of the Church in Western America and its enlarged and successful colonization there. In the progress of the Lord's work the crossing of phase lines can be painful but necessary.

The members of The Church of Jesus Christ of Latter-day Saints who experience mocking of temple rituals, ridicule of the Book of Mormon, and attempted belittling of the Prophet Joseph Smith can learn from the prison-temple how adversity has its uses. Though it is regrettable that such should come, efforts to weaken the Church will, ironically, only end up by strengthening faithful members and heightening their appreciation for temples, scriptures, and prophets.

In the progress now being made along the "decreed course" of the Church, prophecies are meanwhile being fulfilled. Among the decreed outcomes (underscored by the determined "shalls" of divine communication) are several which emanated from the prison-temple.

First, "A seer *shall* the Lord my God raise up . . ." said ancient Joseph (2 Nephi 3:6; italics added).

Second, "other books" (1 Nephi 13:39, 40) with pages and pages of scripture, as promised, have come forth and "*shall* establish the truth" of the Bible. These other books came almost exclusively through the Prophet Joseph, to be conjoined with the Holy Bible. Now, as never before—now all these scriptures "*shall* grow together" (2 Nephi 3:12; italics added).

Third, as enemies try to destroy the work of Joseph they have been and "*shall* be confounded" (2 Nephi 3:14; italics added). (See chapter 3.)

Fourth, as Joseph was assured in Liberty Jail, "thy people *shall* never be turned against thee by the testimony of traitors" (D&C 122:3; italics added).

Fifth, as promised the Prophet-prisoner so stunningly and accurately in that obscure frontier jail, "The ends of the earth *shall* inquire after thy name" (D&C 122:1; italics added).

It is hoped that earnest readers will come away from looking through this witnessing "window" not only with greater appreciation for imperfect but improving Joseph as a "choice seer" (chapter 2) but also with a greater determination to meet the demands of their own discipleship in our time and amid our own vexations.

Though on the scale of global significance our tutoring experiences are smaller than the Prophet's, the insights, principles, and doctrines discussed herein apply to all of us. As our individual premortal[5] preparation is linked to our mortal refining, we too are told to "endure it well."

Furthermore, the same converging and consolidating of doctrines and experience manifest by Joseph in jail need to occur in each of us. Our own mix, too, of mortality and adversity "shall be but for a small moment"—but what an important moment!

May we use that moment well.

Notes

1. The author expresses deep appreciation to Al Rounds for permission to so use his painting, but most of all for the way in which he is using his talents in producing Restoration art.

2. Joseph had been very close to Liberty, Missouri, before; it was a few miles from there that the men of Zion's Camp ended their march in 1834, smitten by cholera. Of that march, the author has said: "God is more concerned with growth than with geography. Thus, those who marched in Zion's Camp were not exploring the Missouri countryside but their own possibilities." (Conference Report, October 1976, p. 16.)

3. Significantly, faithful and able Hyrum, his older brother, was at Joseph's side in both jails.

4. Three at Crooked River—including David W. Patten, one of the Twelve —and seventeen at Haun's Mill.

5. In this volume, the word *premortal* is preferred to the more commonly used *preexistence*. The spirit element of the individual soul is eternal and therefore could not have existed before it existed.

CHAPTER 1

"Thine Adversity . . . Shall Be But a Small Moment" *D&C 121:7*

For the Prophet Joseph Smith, the experience in Liberty Jail was a time not only of suffering but also of reflecting which led to a further consolidating and integrating of his thinking. This converging process involved what he had previously learned as well as what he was then learning. Incarcerated Joseph wrote that "the things of God are of deep import and time and experience and careful and ponderous and solemn thoughts can only find them out" (*Writings*, p. 396). Joseph's Spirit-aided learning involved what Paul had likewise called "the deep things of God" (1 Corinthians 2:10).

The whole experience in Liberty Jail, as Joseph indicated, was such that without it he could not possibly have understood certain dimensions of suffering. It was just as promised in an 1834 blessing given him by his father:[1] "Thy heart shall meditate great wisdom and comprehend the deep things of God" (Father's Blessing, 1834). In the prison-temple Joseph was being shown even more deeply "things as they really are, and . . . things as they really will be" (Jacob 4:13), words he had translated nearly a decade before.

The peculiar "vantage point" even prompted Joseph to view with some objectivity the refiner's fire, not only as it affected him but as it affected his people as well: from the prison-temple, in his epistle to the Church, he observed that "God hath said that he would have a tried people" (*Writings*, p. 395).

This reference in the March 1839 epistle about the Lord's

developing a "tried people," purged as gold in a crucible, found later confirmation in a revelation given to President Brigham Young in January 1847 at Winter Quarters: "My people must be tried in all things, that they may be prepared to receive the glory that I have for them, even the glory of Zion; and he that will not bear chastisement is not worthy of my kingdom" (D&C 136:31).

Joseph's words from jail and the latter words, given after the exodus from the City of Joseph, reflect another tutorial reality as translated by Joseph Smith years before: "Nevertheless the Lord seeth fit to chasten his people; yea, he trieth their patience and their faith" (Mosiah 23:21).

Through all that comprised the experience in the prison-temple, Joseph remained confident that the work would roll on, because "God is . . . our shield, . . . it was by his voice that we were called to a dispensation of his gospel in the beginning of the fulness of times. It was by him we received the Book of Mormon." (*Writings*, pp. 398–99.)[2]

As the hectic earlier years gave way to enforced confinement in Liberty Jail, there was time to reflect deeply. Peter's words come to mind which suggest that God would, "after that ye have suffered a while, make you perfect, stablish, strengthen, settle you" (1 Peter 5:10).

Imprisoned Joseph, in fact, noted that certain remedies are to be acquired only by "time and experience." Doubtless this realization and the Prophet's consciousness that he was being tutored underwrote his vow: "We are determined to endure tribulation as good soldiers unto the end" (*Writings*, p. 399). Understandably, he shared the feelings of Paul—"Who shall separate us from the love of Christ? shall tribulation, or distress, or persecution, or famine, or nakedness, or peril, or sword?" (Romans 8:35)—when he wrote, "Nothing therefore can separate us from the love of God" (*Writings*, p. 390). Besides, the perils through which Joseph was called to pass "seem but a small thing to me" (D&C 127:2).

In the midst of his adversity, there came one of the most sublime and significant revelations ever received by Joseph or any other prophet—that now numbered sections 121 and 122 of the Doctrine and Covenants. These revelations are so invested with rich truths that any focusing on one portion is apt, even unintentionally, to neglect another.

The doctrine of man's premortal existence—"things as they really were"—was further ripened in Joseph while he was in the prison-temple, and he was made ready for further public expression about it. (See chapters 4 and 5 of this book.)

It is not surprising that the Lord, whose plans Joseph was carrying out, would reassure him that he would not be taken before his time[3] (see D&C 122:9). All men have a time appointed when we will stand before the judgment bar of God. It is the author's opinion that each of us mortals has a time frame appointed within which we are permitted to do our work in this world (see Alma 12:27; D&C 42:48; 121:25). "Revelations" and "things" occur in their times (see D&C 59:4; 64:32); so also with people.

Furthermore, there had been revealed to Joseph seven years earlier the future of those not valiant in the testimony of Jesus (see D&C 76:79). That revelation can be juxtaposed to what the Prophet was told while in the jail: "endure it well," for glorious promises were given to those "who have endured valiantly for the gospel of Jesus Christ" (D&C 121:29). Even if otherwise "honorable," those who are not valiant in the testimony of Jesus cannot be crowned in the celestial kingdom. A "good soldier" is "valiant" to the end.

The tutoring but sobering summation "all these things shall give thee experience, and shall be for thy good" (D&C 122:7)[4] is most assuredly the major development theme which emerges from the prison-temple. This tutorial theme received even further application in the deepened understanding which came to the incarcerated Joseph: the Lord revealed to him the substance and style—in essence "what manner of men" (3 Nephi 27:27)— he desires those who hold his holy priesthood to be. (See D&C 121:34–46.)

This transcendent revelation, so profound as to constitute a towering witness to Joseph Smith's prophetic powers, is in effect an amplification of a terse verse in the New Testament, "For many are called, but few are chosen" (Matthew 22:14):

Behold, there are many called, but few are chosen. And why are they not chosen?

Because their hearts are set so much upon the things of this world, and aspire to the honors of men, that they do not learn this one lesson—

That the rights of the priesthood are inseparably connected with the powers of heaven, and that the powers of heaven cannot be controlled nor handled only upon the principles of righteousness.

That they may be conferred upon us, it is true; but when we undertake to cover our sins, or to gratify our pride, our vain ambition, or to exercise control or dominion or compulsion upon the souls of the children of men, in any degree of unrighteousness, behold, the heavens withdraw themselves; the Spirit of the Lord is grieved; and when it is withdrawn, Amen to the priesthood or the authority of that man.

Behold, ere he is aware, he is left unto himself, to kick against the pricks, to persecute the saints, and to fight against God.

.We have learned by sad experience that it is the nature and disposition of almost all men, as soon as they get a little authority, as they suppose, they will immediately begin to exercise unrighteous dominion.

Hence many are called, but few are chosen. (D&C 121:34–40.)

Thus at the very time he was suffering telestial abuse and oppression from secular authorities ranging from judges to jailers, Joseph was instructed on the completely opposite manner, the celestial way, in which the Lord's priesthood leaders are to lead!

No power or influence can or ought to be maintained by virtue of the priesthood, only by persuasion, by long-suffering, by gentleness and meekness, and by love unfeigned;

By kindness, and pure knowledge, which shall greatly enlarge the soul without hypocrisy, and without guile—

Reproving betimes with sharpness, when moved upon by the Holy Ghost; and then showing forth afterwards an increase of love toward him whom thou hast reproved, lest he esteem thee to be his enemy. (D&C 121:41–43.)

Obviously this supernal spiritual style of leadership as thus set forth could not be sustained for long by anyone who was casual in his commitment or who was not making significant spiritual strides in developing the attributes of Jesus. This leadership style and attitude here made specific to priesthood bearers matched the attributes and qualities of a true Saint noted in precious lines translated by Joseph Smith a decade before: "and becometh a saint . . . and becometh as a child, submissive, meek, humble, patient, full of love, willing to submit to all things which the Lord seeth fit to inflict upon him, even as a child doth submit to his father" (Mosiah 3:19).

The rigorousness of such requirements is clear, but it is matched by the richness of the Lord's promise:

> Let thy bowels also be full of charity towards all men, and to the household of faith, and let virtue garnish thy thoughts unceasingly; then shall thy confidence wax strong in the presence of God; and the doctrine of the priesthood shall distil upon thy soul as the dews from heaven.
>
> The Holy Ghost shall be thy constant companion, and thy scepter an unchanging scepter of righteousness and truth; and thy dominion shall be an everlasting dominion, and without compulsory means it shall flow unto thee forever and ever. (D&C 121:45, 46.)

Though he was in an obscure and dismal dungeon, for Joseph the pointed tutoring and rich revealing continued—accompanied by striking promises of much more revelation to come to the Lord's prophets and people, revelation about "things as they really will be," for there would be

> A time to come in the which nothing shall be withheld, whether there be one God or many gods, they shall be manifest. . . .
>
> According to that which was ordained in the midst of the Council of the Eternal God of all other gods before this world was, that should be reserved unto the finishing and the end thereof, when every man shall enter into his eternal presence and into his immortal rest. (D&C 121: 28, 32.)

Separated from them though he was, Joseph was further assured that the people of the Church "shall never be turned against [him] by the testimony of traitors" (D&C 122:3). It is a comfort that this promise is as valid today as when it was given in March of 1839. Such defectors and other detractors caused trouble then (see D&C 122:4) as they do now. Nevertheless such troubles and afflictions, comparatively speaking, will be "but for a small moment" (D&C 122:4; see also 2 Corinthians 4:17).

Joseph, "called to pass through tribulation," would thereby come to understand "according to the flesh" (see Alma 7:11–12), what it was like to be "cast into the pit" (D&C 122:5, 7). This expression was reminiscent of another Joseph, the son of Jacob: "And they took him, and cast him into a pit: and the pit was empty, there was no water in it" (Genesis 37:24).

Significantly, ancient Joseph prophesied that Joseph Smith, Jr., "shall be like unto me" (2 Nephi 3:15). (See chapter 6 for comparisons.)

The four-word preamble to the Lord's summational lines given to the Prophet Joseph in jail concerning the development of discipleship is affectingly tender: "Know thou, my son" (D&C 122:7). However, a solemn array of difficulties the Prophet had already undergone (D&C 122:5–7) as representative of others that might still be required of him, preceded those reassuring lines. Nevertheless, "all these things shall give thee experience, and shall be for thy good," providing Joseph "endured it well" and "valiantly."

This great revelation closed by noting that Jesus had "descended below" all things. Joseph was certainly not greater than he, so Joseph was to be Job-like and "hold on thy way." (D&C 122:8–9.)

What a pointed and powerful reminder about Jesus' being our model! Once more, later revelation was affirming earlier directive words Joseph had translated ten years before, when perhaps he had not fully realized their developmental implications.

> Therefore I would that ye should be perfect even as I, or your Father who is in heaven is perfect (3 Nephi 12:48).

> Therefore, what manner of men ought ye to be? Verily I say unto you, even as I am. (3 Nephi 27:27.)

Yes, Liberty Jail was an awful dungeon, but it was also a truly tutoring temple.

Section 123, also written from prison, shows the converging of Joseph's memories and experiences. For instance, he employed an analogy used by James about how a small helm can benefit a large ship (D&C 123:16; see also James 3:4).

In this section the Prophet, writing to the Saints, urged a cataloging of the injustices they had experienced in the Missouri persecutions[5] and noted what an iniquitous world it was. (See verse 7.) Nevertheless, Joseph was so committed to his calling that he and others were willing to wear out their lives. Why? Because, wrote this truth-telling prophet, we have "an imperative duty" to those on the earth "who are only kept from the truth because they know not where to find it" (verses 11–13).

In the timing and wisdom of the Lord, the schooling revelations of March 1839 were given when the Prophet was fully ready to receive them. They were not given just after the First Vision, or even a decade earlier during Joseph's remarkable translation of the Book of Mormon. Schooling has its seasons, even for prophets.

Just as rugged but remote mountains in the Sinai were the scene of very significant preparational moments in the life of Moses, so a rock-hewn jail in Missouri was the obscure, unlikely site of marvelous nurturing revelations from God to a modern prophet and his people. Joseph's time "in this solitary place" (*Writings*, p. 375) provided such a useful interval.

In a December 16, 1838, letter to the Saints, Joseph wrote, "Do not think that our hearts faint as though some strange thing had happened unto us" (*Writings*, p. 375). In this we see the deepening and further developing of his own discipleship as he obviously drew upon Peter's words: "Beloved, think it not strange concerning the fiery trial which is to try you, as though some strange thing happened unto you" (1 Peter 4:12).

Likewise Joseph cited the words of Isaiah (see Isaiah 29:21) and Nephi (see 2 Nephi 27:32), "Men have laid snares for us, we have spoken words and men have made us offenders"; the analogy of "Job's comforters" (see Job 16:2); and John's lament (see Revelation 6:9) about what can happen in consequence of one's bearing the testimony of Jesus Christ (*Writings*, pp. 376–77).

The Prophet may have recalled Judas, too, for he observed that "Mormon dissenters" were being used "against us," because such misguided souls were "thinking thereby to gain the friendship of the world." Ironically, those of the world who used such dissenters would end up, said Joseph to the Church in this epistle, hating "them worse than they do us because they find them to be base traitors and sycophants." (*Writings*, p. 379.) This was a foreshadowing of verses to be received several months later: "those that shall lift up the heel against mine anointed [saying] they have sinned when they have not sinned . . . and those who swear falsely against my servants . . . , they themselves shall be despised by those that flattered them" (D&C 121: 16, 18, 20). Judas knew what it was to be used and then despised (see Matthew 27:3–5).

In a March 15, 1839, letter sent from jail Joseph made significant linkage with his prophet-predecessors: "[but trials] will only give us that knowledge to understand the minds of the Ancients. For my part," wrote Joseph, "I think I never could have felt as I now do if I had not suffered the wrongs that I have suffered." (*Writings*, p. 387.) It is a rare person who can appreciate such lessons while the lessons are in process; it takes special perspective.

Joseph's mind even contemplated comparatively ancient Abraham. In his epistle to the Church at Quincy, the Prophet expressed the thought that Abraham and the ancients would "not have whereof to boast over us in the day of judgment as being called to pass through heavier afflictions."[6] These modern disciples could now "hold an even weight in the balances with them." (*Writings*, p. 395.)

Joseph's sufferings, however, were too real to be mere philosophical calisthenics. Near the end of his confinement he wrote to Emma, "my nerve trembles from long confinement but if you feel as I do you don't care for the imperfections of my writings" (*Writings*, p. 409).

Joseph's experiences were anything but abstract. "We are kept under a strong guard, night and day, in a prison of double walls and doors . . . ; our food is scant, uniform, and coarse; we have not the privilege of cooking for ourselves, we have been compelled to sleep on the floor with straw, and not blankets sufficient to keep us warm; and when we have a fire, we are obliged to have almost a constant smoke" (*Writings*, pp. 417–18).

Recantation by Joseph would have meant liberation. Yet Joseph and the others would not deny their religion simply because of oppression: "We have never dissembled, nor will we for the sake of our lives" (*Writings*, p. 376). "But if we will deny our religion, we can be liberated" (*Writings*, p. 418). Instead, they

would "hold on until death" because "God is true . . . the Constitution of the United States is [true], . . . the Bible is true, . . .
the Book of Mormon is true [and] the Book of Covenants . . . ;
Christ is true [and his] ministering angels" (*Writings*, p. 407). By
the time of his imprisonment, Joseph had had significant personal experiences concerning the specifics of which he so testified. Still, he and the others found themselves "wearing away
very fast" (*Writings*, p. 419).

A day or two before his release, in a poignant letter written at
sunset (April 4, 1839), Joseph looked through the bars "of this
lonesome prison" with his full emotions "known only to God."
He wrote that his contemplations defied description by pen or
tongue. How could he describe his feelings to others "who never
experienced what we experience"? (*Writings*, p. 425.) The necessary role of such experience had, after all, been cited by Joseph's
divine mentor just a few days before (see D&C 122:7).

In this his last letter to Emma from Liberty Jail, he said he
wished to act upon the "principle of generosity." His generosity
amid adversity would not have been fully possible without the
relevant experiences or Joseph's capacity to "hear instruction,
and be wise, and refuse it not" (Proverbs 8:33).

Thus, just as Jesus grew in wisdom and in stature and in favor
with God and man (Luke 1:80; 2:40, 52; see also 1 Samuel 2:26),
so did Joseph Smith, this development being enhanced by the
suffering in Liberty Jail. Jesus' obedience was perfected by his
suffering (Hebrews 5:8–9). For Joseph Smith, suffering increased
his obedience.

The struggle is intense along the pathway to perfection, yet it
is a trek necessitated by Jesus' having asked us to become "even
as I am" (3 Nephi 27:27). Through the Prophet Joseph Smith,
either by translation or revelation, great insights came concerning
this deepening of one's discipleship.

The Holy Bible, with its apostolic witness, reflects some of
these same illuminating insights about the exacting requirements
involved in the development of discipleship. From biblical state-
ments it is clear that, while perfection is a very distant goal, it is
not an unthinkable goal. Moreover, customized challenges are required:

Jesus said unto him, If thou wilt be perfect, go and sell that thou hast, and give to the poor, and thou shalt have treasure in heaven: and come and follow me (Matthew 19:21).

The disciple is not above his master: but every one that is perfect shall be as his master (Luke 6:40).

And that which fell among thorns are they, which, when they have heard, go forth, and are choked with cares and riches and pleasures of this life, and bring no fruit to perfection (Luke 8:14).

For the perfecting of the Saints, for the work of the ministry, for the edifying of the body of Christ (Ephesians 4:12).

Night and day praying exceedingly that we might see your face, and might perfect that which is lacking in your faith (1 Thessalonians 3:10).

Seeing then that all these things shall be dissolved, what manner of persons ought ye to be in all holy conversation and godliness (2 Peter 3:11).

Yea, and all that will live godly in Christ Jesus shall suffer persecution (2 Timothy 3:12).

Wherefore let them that suffer according to the will of God commit the keeping of their souls to him in well doing, as unto a faithful Creator (1 Peter 4:19).

Among the remarkable latter-day scriptures further illuminating this heartland of serious discipleship are these, all of which came through Joseph by revelation or translation, including two during his incarceration:

Nevertheless the Lord seeth fit to chasten his people; yea, he trieth their patience and their faith (Mosiah 23:21).

Ye are not able to abide the presence of God now, neither the ministering of angels; wherefore, continue in patience until ye are perfected (D&C 67:13).

And if men come unto me I will show unto them their weakness. I give unto men weakness that they may be humble; and my grace is sufficient for all men that humble themselves before me; for if they humble themselves before me, and have faith in me, then will I make weak things become strong unto them. (Ether 12:27.)

. . . and becometh as a child, submissive, meek, humble, patient, full of love, willing to submit to all things which the Lord seeth fit to inflict upon him, even as a child doth submit to his father (Mosiah 3:19).

And out of weakness he shall be made strong, in that day when my work shall commence among all my people, unto the restoring thee, O house of Israel, saith the Lord (2 Nephi 3:13).

My son, peace be unto thy soul; thine adversity and thine afflictions shall be but a small moment (D&C 121:7).

And if thou shouldst be cast into the pit, or into the hands of murderers, and the sentence of death passed upon thee; if thou be cast into the deep, if the billowing surge conspire against thee; if fierce winds become thine enemy; if the heavens gather blackness, and all the elements combine to hedge up the way; and above all, if the very jaws of hell shall gape open the mouth wide after thee, know thou, my son, that all these things shall give thee experience, and shall be for thy good (D&C 122:7).

The abundance and relevance of these and other doctrines which flowed through Joseph constitute major reasons why our Lord foretellingly told him, "The ends of the earth shall inquire after thy name" (D&C 122:1). So far as we know, much more scripture flowed through the Prophet Joseph than through any other mortal in history, giving ample reason for such inquiry.

In choosing Joseph Smith, the Lord clearly chose one who by the world's standards was formally unlearned and uneducated. He was certainly not sought out initially by others. In so choosing him, the Lord illustrated how much could be done through him, giving us one of the most remarkable selection and utilization lessons in human history.

There was another factor at work in the soul stretching of the Prophet in the Missouri dungeon. Earlier, Joseph had Oliver Cowdery and Sidney Rigdon to be not only his *aides-de-camp* but also in a measure as his spokesmen. After the Liberty Jail experience, however, Joseph was clearly his own spokesman. From that time forward, we begin to receive Joseph's stretching sermons, involving some of the gospel's most powerful doctrines.

Considering Joseph's task-filled and burdening prophetic role, it is little wonder that the Lord told ancient Joseph that his busy namesake, the latter-day seer, would be asked to "do none other work" (2 Nephi 3:8).

Of this latter-day seer it is recorded, "out of weakness he shall be made strong" (2 Nephi 3:13). Father Smith promised his son that one day he would "stand before the Lord, having produced a hundred-fold" (Father's Blessing, 1834). The foregoing words are worth pondering as the effects of the work done by Joseph burgeon across the planet.

Individuals and settings of obscurity are not unusual to the Lord's purposes. Meridian-day Christianity was initiated on a very small geographical scale and with comparatively few people. The larger, busy world paid little heed to it. Likewise with the Book of Mormon peoples. Whether located in Meso-America or elsewhere, they were one people among many peoples on this planet and perhaps even on the western hemisphere. Lack of knowledge of and communication with others was the factor here.

It was thus also, geographically and numerically, on America's western frontier. Palmyra was not Paris, and Nauvoo was not New York. Nevertheless, Liberty Jail doubtless resembled other jails and other dungeons which have held other prophets. But in the years ahead, as "the ends of the earth shall inquire after [Joseph's] name," Liberty Jail will loom ever larger in the spiritual history of mankind.

Significantly, Joseph was finally released from Liberty Jail, with a subsequent escape en route, on April 6, 1839—both the Savior's and his church's birthday (D&C 20:1). Though Joseph would have been unaware of it, it was also Passover time, often the celebration of the occasion when ancient Israel was spared from the angel of death and released from bondage![7]

Notes

1. The foretelling and paralleling verses in 2 Nephi 3 and the prescient father's blessing are remarkable, but no more so than the Prophet Joseph's capacity to fulfill them.

2. Joseph's special, post–Liberty Jail desire to see that the Book of Mormon not be neglected was genuine. This is evidenced in what might be called the "Philadelphia Story," late in 1839. Parley P. Pratt, a fellow prisoner in the jail in Richmond prior to Joseph's Liberty Jail experience, related: "While visiting with brother Joseph in Philadelphia, a very large church was opened for him to preach in, and about three thousand people assembled to hear him. Brother [Sidney] Rigdon spoke first, and dwelt on the Gospel, illustrating his

doctrine by the Bible. When he was through, brother Joseph arose like a lion about to roar; and being full of the Holy Ghost, spoke in great power, bearing testimony of the visions he had seen, the ministering of angels which he had enjoyed; and how he had found the plates of the Book of Mormon, and translated them by the gift and power of God. He commenced by saying: 'If nobody else had the courage to testify of so glorious a message from Heaven, and of the finding of so glorious a record, he felt to do it in justice to the people, and leave the event with God.' The entire congregation was astounded; electrified, as it were, and overwhelmed with the sense of the truth and power by which he spoke, and the wonders which he related. A lasting impression was made; many souls were gathered into the fold. And I bear witness, that he, by his faithful and powerful testimony, cleared his garments of their blood." (Pratt, *Autobiography of Parley P. Pratt* [Salt Lake City: Deseret Book Co., 1972], pp. 298–99.)

3. President Brigham Young, who visited Joseph in Liberty Jail, said, "I heard Joseph say many a time, 'I shall not live until I am forty years of age.' " (*Discourses of Brigham Young*, p. 467.) President Wilford Woodruff's journal records that Lyman Wight "said that Joseph told him, while in Liberty Jail, Missouri in 1839, he would not live to see forty years." (*History of the Church* 7:212.) Joseph's accelerated efforts thereafter to prepare the Twelve, including those in early 1844, would have reflected this timetable.

4. In Joseph's letter from Liberty Jail to a Sister Presendia Huntington Buell, dated March 15, 1839, he observed that "all things shall work together for good to them that love God" (*Writings*, p. 387).

5. Clark V. Johnson has tallied the efforts of Church members to secure redress for their miseries in Missouri; 823 petitions signed by 683 petitioners have been found. ("Missouri Persecutions: The Petition of Isaac Leary," *BYU Studies*, vol. 23, no. 1 [Winter 1983], pp. 94–103.)

6. Joseph Smith was not unaware of other developmental comparisons. He later observed (June, 1844) that when God visited with Moses from the bush, "Moses was a stuttering sort of a boy like me" (*Words*, p. 381).

7. April 6, 1839, the day when the Prophet Joseph ended his imprisonment in Liberty Jail, was marked by another significant event. Heber C. Kimball recorded in his journal that on that day "the following words came to my mind, and the Spirit said unto me, 'write,' which I did by taking a piece of paper and writing on my knee as follows: . . . 'Verily I say unto my servant Heber, thou art my son, in whom I am well pleased; for thou art careful to hearken to my words, and not transgress my law, nor rebel against my servant Joseph Smith, for thou hast a respect to the words of mine anointed, even from the least to the greatest of them; therefore thy name is written in heaven, no more to be blotted out for ever, because of these things." (*Words*, p. 18.) Thus on the very day that Joseph was released from the unjustified imprisonment, one of his loyal, leading associates received this splendid assurance from the Lord, ample testimony to how seriously and gratefully the Lord views loyalty to His servants.

CHAPTER 2

"A Choice Seer" 2 Nephi 3:7

ncient Joseph saw the latter-day Joseph in vision and prophetically described him as "a choice seer" (2 Nephi 3:6–7).

We have already noted the Prophet's immense revelatory output. Even prior to Liberty Jail, through inspired translation and direct revelation he had indeed served as an unusually productive seer, probably bringing forth more scripture than any single prophet in history. Being "choice" thus denoted, among other things, being favored as a human conduit for a flood of truth.

Following this initial torrent of truth, imprisoned Joseph bore fervent testimony of those revelations and translations, particularly of the truthfulness of the Book of Mormon: "it was by [God] we received the Book of Mormon"; likewise "the Book of Covenants" (*Writings*, pp. 399, 407).

These two volumes, which came through this "choice seer," are of course among the "other books" of restorative scripture which were prophesied to come forth in the latter days (1 Nephi 13:39–40), while other revelations (including sections 121 and 122 of the Doctrine and Covenants, given in Liberty Jail) would be later added to the storehouse of scripture given through the modern seer. Much of the laying of the scriptural foundation had been already accomplished by Joseph prior to his confinement in Missouri. Only 9 of the total of 133 sections of scripture given through Joseph came in the final period between Liberty and Carthage jails.

To appreciate fully what occurred in Liberty Jail and subsequently as it affected the Prophet Joseph, it is therefore necessary to assess and ponder anew what had come through this "choice seer" *before* the Missouri experience. Only then can one fully savor the significance of the revelations given in March of 1839 and the further spiritual preparations which the Prophet underwent in the months of his confinement in the prison-temple.

While imperfect record-keeping may account for some of Joseph's apparent lack of earlier stress upon the Book of Mormon, comparatively speaking, the Liberty Jail period marked something of a turning point. From the jail Joseph declared the truthfulness of the Book and testified that it had come from God. Perhaps in his ponderings in prison he sensed as never before the converging as well as convincing powers of these "other books." After as well as during the inhumane incarceration, Joseph repeatedly spoke of the Book of Mormon. In November 1841 he described the book as the "keystone" of our religion (*History of the Church,* 4:461). He also urged the Book of Mormon as the "means of doing much good"[1] (*Words,* p. 31).

In the times ahead those who have faith in the Lord's "key of knowledge," "the fulness of the scriptures" (Luke 11:53, JST) will come to even greater appreciation of what a "choice seer" Joseph was. Appreciation of and scholarship concerning these seer-borne scriptures will grow as never before.

An angel told Nephi nearly 2,500 years ago that "other books" of scripture would come forth in the last dispensation, through "a choice seer," to "establish[2] the truth of" the blessed Bible (1 Nephi 13:39–40; 2 Nephi 3:7, 11). Concerning all these books, Joseph testified more than once from Liberty Jail.

The other books of scripture which came through Joseph will yet end up—in additional ways—establishing the truth of the Holy Bible. How fitting, since it was a verse on the precious pages of that book (James 1:5) in which Joseph found the spiritual stimulus to go to the Sacred Grove in 1820!

Yet, sad to say, these reaffirming and clarifying "other books" of scripture—laden with plain and precious truths—have been, are, and will be denigrated by many, drawing the scorner's sting. Moreover, fascination with the environment in which the

Book of Mormon came forth has caused some to neglect its content. Likewise, the *human-ness* of those associated with its emergence has caused neglect of the *divine-ness* of its message.

This coming forth of other books of scripture was, in fact,
miraculously accomplished—by both translation and revelation
—through a "choice seer," the Prophet Joseph Smith. Even so,
the richness of the Book of Mormon, for instance, has been
missed by critics and casual Church members alike. They fail to
see that both the intricacy and the simplicity of the book are
beyond the capacity of any mortal being to produce, including
Joseph Smith. What came *through* Joseph was *beyond* him and
stretched him!

Joseph was instead that rarity in human history, a translating
seer: "And you have a gift to translate the plates; and this is the
first gift that I bestowed upon you; and I have commanded that
you should pretend to no other gift until my purpose is fulfilled in
this; for I will grant unto you no other gift until it is finished. . . .
But this generation shall have my word through you." (D&C 5:4,
10.)

Anciently it was understood how rarely this high "gift from
God" is given:

> Now Ammon said unto him: I can assuredly tell thee, O king,
> of a man that can translate the records; for he has wherewith that he
> can look, and translate all records that are of ancient date; and it is a
> gift from God. And the things are called interpreters, and no man
> can look in them except he be commanded, lest he should look for
> that he ought not and he should perish. And whosoever is
> commanded to look in them, the same is called seer. . . .
>
> Thus God has provided a means that man, through faith, might
> work mighty miracles; therefore he becometh a great benefit to his
> fellow beings. (Mosiah 8:13, 18.)

In the aggregate, these fruits of Joseph's labors constitute a
massive contribution, one reason why those who try to destroy
the work of this seer are both confounded and diverted (see 2
Nephi 3:14).

Furthermore these "other books," particularly the Book of
Mormon, "make known . . . plain and precious" truths some of
which do not appear as fully in the Bible. Some truths were, long
ago, "kept back" from the later translation process through

which we received the Holy Bible. (See 1 Nephi 13:32, 34, 40.) As Robert Matthews has said, it is more a deficiency of *transmission* than of *translation*. Whatever the earlier deficiencies, through the Restoration these precious truths would be "had again" among as many "as shall believe" (Moses 1:41).

The return of such truths to the earth features simplicity. The faithful Book of Mormon peoples' straightforward "cry from the dust . . . after many generations . . . shall go, even according to the *simpleness of their words*. Because of *their faith their words* shall proceed forth . . . unto . . . the fruit of thy loins; and the *weakness of their words will I make strong in their [posterity's] faith*, unto the remembering of my covenant . . ." (2 Nephi 3:20–21; italics added).

The recognition of the Book of Mormon by Lehi's posterity is even aided by the "simpleness" and "weakness" of its language. The Lord's sheep know his voice (see John 10:16, 27). The resonance is real.

These "other books" provide afresh a much-needed witness that Jesus is the Christ, that the resurrection which was brought about through his atonement is a reality, and that a loving Father-God has a plan of salvation for all mortals. These are transcendent truths—crucial, not incidental.

Another way to measure the revelatory flow through the "choice seer," the Prophet Joseph Smith, is to select a particular topic, such as the one to follow, and compare what came through him (left-hand column) with other precious words from the remarkable Apostles John and Paul (right-hand column). What follows pertains to a dimension of the Second Coming and certain of its accompanying events.

And there shall be silence in heaven for the space of half an hour; and immediately after shall the curtain of heaven be unfolded, as a scroll is unfolded after it is rolled up, and the face of the Lord shall be unveiled;

And the heaven departed as a scroll when it is rolled together; and every mountain and island were moved out of their places (Revelation 6:14).

For what is our hope, or joy, or crown of rejoicing? Are

And the saints that are upon the earth, who are alive, shall be quickened and be caught up to meet him.

And they who have slept in their graves shall come forth, for their graves shall be opened; and they also shall be caught up to meet him in the midst of the pillar of heaven—

They are Christ's, the first fruits, they who shall descend with him first, and they who are on the earth and in their graves, who are first caught up to meet him; and all this by the voice of the sounding of the trump of the angel of God.

And after this another angel shall sound, which is the second trump; and then cometh the redemption of those who are Christ's at his coming; who have received their part in that prison which is prepared for them, that they might receive the gospel, and be judged according to men in the flesh.

And again, another trump shall sound, which is the third trump; and then come the spirits of men who are to be judged, and are found under condemnation;

And these are the rest of the dead; and they live not again until the thousand years are ended, neither again, until the end of the earth.

And another trump shall sound, which is the fourth

not even ye in the presence of our Lord Jesus Christ at his coming? (1 Thessalonians 2:19.)

For the Lord himself shall descend from heaven with a shout, with the voice of the archangel, and with the trump of God: and the dead in Christ shall rise first:

Then we which are alive and remain shall be caught up together with them in the clouds, to meet the Lord in the air: and so shall we ever be with the Lord. (1 Thessalonians 4:16–17.)

But every man in his own order: Christ the firstfruits; afterward they that are Christ's at his coming (1 Corinthians 15:23).

And the sea gave up the dead which were in it; and death and hell delivered up the dead which were in them: and they were judged every man according to their works (Revelation 20:13).

trump, saying: There are found among those who are to remain until that great and last day, even the end, who shall remain filthy still.

And another trump shall sound, which is the fifth trump, which is the fifth angel who committeth the everlasting gospel—flying through the midst of heaven, unto all nations, kindreds, tongues, and people;

And this shall be the sound of his trump, saying to all people, both in heaven and in earth, and that are under the earth—for every ear shall hear it, and every knee shall bow, and every tongue shall confess, while they hear the sound of the trump, saying: Fear God, and give glory to him who sitteth upon the throne, forever and ever; for the hour of his judgment is come. (D&C 88:95–104.)

But the rest of the dead lived not again until the thousand years were finished. This is the first resurrection. (Revelation 20:5.)

And I saw another angel fly in the midst of heaven, having the everlasting gospel to preach unto them that dwell on the earth, and to every nation, and kindred, and tongue, and people (Revelation 14:6).

Incidentally, while the revelation in the left column (now section 88) was given to the Prophet Joseph Smith on December 27, 1832, the recorded examples of his public utterances about these particular things appear mostly in the post–Liberty Jail period.

The revelatory outpouring from the "choice seer" also had lasting impact on Joseph's true friends and followers. Hugh Nibley observed: "Before he met Joseph Smith, Brigham recalls, 'the secret feeling of my heart was that I would be willing to crawl around the earth on my hands and knees, to see such a man as was Peter, Jeremiah, Moses, or any man that could tell me anything about God and heaven. . . . When I saw Joseph Smith, he took heaven figuratively speaking, and brought it down to earth; and he took the earth, brought it up, and opened up, in plainness and simplicity, the things of God; and that is the beauty of his mission." (*Timely and Timeless,* p. 234.)

While he was not easily impressed by anyone, President Young's regard for Joseph was deep and it never left him. Of his pupil-prophet relationship with Joseph he said, "An angel never watched him closer than I did, and that is what has given me the knowledge I have today. I treasure it up, and ask the Father in the name of Jesus, to help my memory when information is wanted." (Brigham Young Papers, October 8, 1866, sermon.)

On another occasion, Brigham Young said, "I feel like shouting 'Hallelujah!' all the time when I think that I ever knew Joseph Smith, the Prophet" (*Journal of Discourses* 3:51). Significantly, Brigham Young's last mortal words were, "Joseph, Joseph, Joseph."

Sequentially, Brigham Young encountered the Book of Mormon first, then its translator.

The Book of Mormon's emergence was remarkable, as Isaiah's imagery foretold: "And thou shalt be brought down, and shalt speak out of the ground, and thy speech shall be low out of the dust, and thy voice shall be, as of one that hath a familiar spirit, out of the ground, and thy speech shall whisper out of the dust" (Isaiah 29:4).

What actually happened was consistent with the Lord's declared intentions:

> And for this very purpose are these plates preserved, which contain these records—that the promises of the Lord might be fulfilled, which he made to his people;
> And that the Lamanites might come to the knowledge of their fathers, and that they might know the promises of the Lord, and that they may believe the gospel and rely upon the merits of Jesus Christ, and be glorified through faith in his name, and that through their repentance they might be saved. Amen. (D&C 3:19–20.)

Truly, all these additional books of holy scripture have come to us in a unique way. For instance, the contents of the Book of Mormon have been supplied by about two dozen prophet-leaders; the editing was done, primarily, by three prophet-historians; and the final translation was performed by the Prophet Joseph Smith. Joseph Smith had the unusual gift of translation given to only a select few prophets (see Mosiah 8:12–18; 28:11–16; D&C 1:29).

Beneficial and wonderful as the Holy Bible is, it did not encompass the same consistent pattern of emergence as the Book of Mormon, with prophets at every stage—*writing, selecting, editing,* and *translating.*

There are even special portions of the Book of Mormon, the Doctrine and Covenants, and the Pearl of Great Price which represent, as it were, "implants" of whole blocks of precious truth which can transport us outside and beyond the brief and tiny place we presently occupy in time and space. As Richard L. Bushman has written, "In some passages the Book of Mormon and the Book of Moses appear to come from another world entirely" (Bushman, p. 77).

Ironically, there has often been more discussion as to the "origins" of these scriptures than about the precious truths they contain.

Though published for decades, some of these truths still have not received our full appreciation. Perhaps similar neglect was a part of the reason for the condemnation the Church received from the Lord in 1832 because, among other things, the Book of Mormon had been treated "lightly" (see D&C 84:54, 57).

For some Church members the Book of Mormon remains unread. Others use it occasionally as if it were merely a handy book of quotations. Still others accept and read it but do not really explore and ponder it. The book is to be feasted upon, not nibbled (see 2 Nephi 31:20). Apparently Church members were similarly spread out on the spectrum of utilization and appreciation in Joseph's day—hence his testimony from jail as to the Book of Mormon, his "keystone" statement, and the instructive episode in Philadelphia are even more understandable.

Quite understandably too, among early Church members the use of the Bible was much greater than the use of the Book of Mormon. Even Joseph, who had been schooled in the Bible, had scarcely had time to translate and begin to assimilate the Book of Mormon, let along to articulate extensively regarding the gems in that book of whose truthfulness he testified. The unfolding process by which these scriptures "shall grow together" (2 Nephi

3:12) was, therefore, a gradual development to be accelerated in the second century of the Restoration, such as with the new editions of the scriptures published in 1979 and 1981.

In any event, for centuries the Lord oversaw the painstaking work of prophets engraving, as they did, upon the plates which would be the basis of the Book of Mormon. He could scarcely be true to those diligent men, whom he loved and called, had he ignored the modern Church's casualness about the Book of Mormon. After all, merely holding or reading a menu is not the same thing as eating a fine meal.

Regarding the incredible "implants" which appear in these "other books," one searches in vain for ways to analogize adequately. These are like nuggets found far from the original mine, or like Mount Everest towering above sister peaks. If the transcendent theology in these books were today's high technology, it would suddenly appear, free standing, with only a few loose wires indicating previous connections.

Examples of such Everests would include chapter 3 of Abraham, chapter 1 of Moses, the third and fourth books of Nephi, and of course such verses as D&C 76:24; 107:53–57—and 121:26–32, from Liberty Jail. There are many others. These special portions sometimes stand amid a penumbra of other well-loved, less spectacular chapters and verses of scripture.

There are biblical instances of this sudden richness, too. The record of the wondrous events—full of import—atop the Mount of Transfiguration are one example; more was given there than most Bible readers explore or properly appreciate.

> And after six days Jesus taketh Peter, James, and John his brother, and bringeth them up into an high mountain apart,
>
> And was transfigured before them: and his face did shine as the sun, and his raiment was white as the light.
>
> And, behold, there appeared unto them Moses and Elias talking with him.
>
> Then answered Peter, and said unto Jesus, Lord, it is good for us to be here: if thou wilt, let us make here three tabernacles; one for thee, and one for Moses, and one for Elias.
>
> While he yet spake, behold, a bright cloud overshadowed them: and behold a voice out of the cloud, which said, This is my beloved Son, in whom I am well pleased; hear ye him.

And when the disciples heard it, they fell on their face, and were sore afraid.

And Jesus came and touched them, and said, Arise, and be not afraid.

And when they had lifted up their eyes, they saw no man, save Jesus only. (Matthew 17:1–8; see also Mark 9:2–10; Luke 9:28–36; and 2 Peter 1:16–18.)

The portent and implications of that regal rendezvous are stunning! Much that was of enormous significance took place then pertaining to the holding of priesthood keys, God's honoring those responsible for dispensational dominions and keys, and the manner in which God tutors and develops his serious disciples (see *Teachings*, p. 158). Such biblical richness, however, often goes unexplored and unattended.

Perhaps too we are given more than we can now fully assess in some biblical verses thus "implanted," such as those that occur after an incident that prompted legalistic concern as to whether Jesus had violated the Sabbath day, and amid questioning by Pharisees.

Then answered Jesus and said unto them, Verily, verily, I say unto you, The Son can do nothing of himself, but what he seeth the Father do: for what things soever he doeth, these also doeth the Son likewise (John 5:19).

Then said Jesus unto them, When ye have lifted up the Son of man, then shall ye know that I am he, and that I do nothing of myself; but as my Father hath taught me, I speak these things (John 8:28).

When God so provides precious verses he does not do so randomly but for "a wise purpose" (see 1 Nephi 9:5; Words of Mormon 1:7; Alma 37:2, 12, 14, 18).

Through the "choice seer" and as nowhere else in holy writ, we are told what God's work and motivation are: "For behold, this is my work and my glory—to bring to pass the immortality and eternal life of man" (Moses 1:39). All the things he does fit into this framework and honor his intent: "He doeth not anything save it be for the benefit of the world; for he loveth the world" (2 Nephi 26:24).

Another such striking example of preeminent verses which came to us through the "choice seer" is King Benjamin's valedictory sermon (about 124 B.C.—Mosiah 2–5). Several centuries after the address, a delighted Mormon discovered this sermon among many other assembled writings. The address is one of the most remarkable sermons on record, and without Joseph Smith's translation it would be lost to us.

> Believe in God; believe that he is, and that he created all things, both in heaven and in earth; believe that he has all wisdom, and all power, both in heaven and in earth; believe that man doth not comprehend all the things which the Lord can comprehend (Mosiah 4:9).

Certain contextual verses on either side of the sermon are useful but not as supernal.

A loving, planning, shepherding God uses his prophets to feed his people. At times he provides especially rich nourishment, causing us to cast our gaze to people and places far beyond the moment at hand:

> And verily I say unto you, that ye are they of whom I said: Other sheep I have which are not of this fold; them also I must bring, and they shall hear my voice; and there shall be one fold, and one shepherd (3 Nephi 15:21).

> And verily, verily, I say unto you that I have other sheep, which are not of this land, neither of the land of Jerusalem, neither in any parts of that land round about whither I have been to minister.
> For they of whom I speak are they who have not as yet heard my voice; neither have I at any time manifested myself unto them.
> But I have received a commandment of the Father that I shall go unto them, and that they shall hear my voice, and shall be numbered among my sheep, that there may be one fold and one shepherd; therefore I go to show myself unto them. (3 Nephi 16:1–3.)

> That by him, and through him, and of him, the worlds are and were created, and the inhabitants thereof are begotten sons and daughters unto God (D&C 76:24).

The Lord even gives exclusive assignments to some prophets to bring forth certain special portions of his word. Once it was John's turn, not Nephi's:

> Wherefore, the things which he shall write are just and true; and behold they are written in the book which thou beheld proceeding out of the mouth of the Jew; and at the time they proceeded

out of the mouth of the Jew, or, at the time the book proceeded out of the mouth of the Jew, the things which were written were plain and pure, and most precious and easy to the understanding of all men. . . .

But the things which thou shalt see hereafter thou shalt not write; for the Lord God hath ordained the apostle of the Lamb of God that he should write them. (1 Nephi 14:23, 25.)

More than most of us have realized, God even honors certain calendric commitments, certain ancient festivals, and certain symbols which likewise transcend time and space.[3]

This should not surprise us.

The resurrected Jesus told the Apostles who had "caught nothing" to cast their empty nets on the right side of the boat, knowing the location of a school of fish at that instant in the sea of Tiberius (John 21:6). The same Lord likewise knows when, where, and how to bring forth fresh spiritual food upon which his followers need to feast (see 2 Nephi 31:20).

Some doctrines among the smorgasbord of scriptures bring to us especially rich and nutritious portions. A great many of these have come in their fulness through Joseph Smith, "a choice seer," and when thoughtfully examined they prove to be "convincing," just as was foreseen (2 Nephi 3:11).

There is thus no democracy of salvational or developmental worth in the words of scripture. In the hierarchy of truth, the truths which came through Joseph are well represented at the apex, including the powerful verities revealed in Liberty Jail.

By way of further example, the worth of the first verse below is greater than the verse of Moroni's which follows, with its lineage history involving five generations.

And if men come unto me I will show unto them their weakness. I give unto men weakness that they may be humble; and my grace is sufficient for all men that humble themselves before me; for if they humble themselves before me, and have faith in me, then will I make weak things become strong unto them. (Ether 12:27.)

And he begat Heth, and Heth lived in captivity all his days. And Heth begat Aaron, and Aaron dwelt in captivity all his days; and he begat Amnigaddah, and Amnigaddah also dwelt in captivity all his days; and he begat Coriantum, and Coriantum dwelt in captivity all his days; and he begat Com. (Ether 10:31.)

The "choice seer" translated both verses.

Sometimes Joseph appears to have been fully aware of receiving or processing "a precious morsel," yet perhaps at other times he was not. Of his receipt in June 1830 of the revelation which became the first chapter of Moses, Joseph wrote, "Amid all the trials and tribulations we had to wade through, the Lord, who well knew our infantile and delicate situation, vouchsafed for us a supply of strength, . . . of which the following was a precious morsel" (as quoted in *The Restoration of Plain and Precious Things*, p. 27).

One day, for instance, we will comprehend more fully the reasons and the "wise purpose" for the lengthy fifth chapter of Jacob, with its extensive analogies as to the tame and wild olive trees. Moreover, we will see why there is such abundant use of material from the prophet Zenos. But for now, we must be patient with the unevenness.

The Lord's overseeing of his prophets as recorders and editors, however, has not been uneven, episodic, or random.

Though some verses are not swollen with salvational significance, even the least provide a feeling for the history, the life, and the times of our ancient counterparts. Hence there is in the Book of Mormon a mixture of inspiration as well as seemingly routine succession (Omni 1:3). Even the seeming humdrum of succession and terse lineage history has its divine uses. Ever present among what came to us through the "choice seer" are evidences of the consuming cares of the then world and of the pathos of the past as some became too concerned with the praise as well as the ways of the world.

Some Book of Mormon prophets had "nothing special to report" or faced disincentives to add further to metallic plates which seemed already full or nearly so. Present, too, was the operating assumption that what was to be transmitted was safely engraved on the larger plates which are yet to come forth:

> And as these plates are small, and as these things are written for the intent of the benefit of our brethren the Lamanites, wherefore, it must needs be that I write a little; but I shall not write the things of my prophesying, nor of my revelations. For what could I write more than my fathers have written? For have not they revealed

the plan of salvation? I say unto you, Yea; and this sufficeth me. (Jarom 1:2.)

Now I, Chemish, write what few things I write, in the same book with my brother; for behold, I saw the last which he wrote, that he wrote it with his own hand; and he wrote it in the day that he delivered them unto me. And after this manner we keep the records, for it is according to the commandments of our fathers. And I make an end.

Behold, I, Abinadom, am the son of Chemish. . . .

And behold, the record of this people is engraven upon plates which is had by the kings, according to the generations; and I know of no revelation save that which has been written, neither prophecy; wherefore, that which is sufficient is written. And I make an end. (Omni 1:9–11.)

In Liberty Jail Joseph used fellow prisoners as scribes, and he did not withhold the "precious morsels" received there.

For many of the people in Book of Mormon times the secular drama must have seemed like a succession of "princes come, princes go, an hour of pomp, an hour of show." There were those then, too, who "lived without God in the world," refusing to be impressed with the divine purposes of life. For such in our time Mother Teresa of Avila has said it well, since, for these, "life is no more than a night in a second-class hotel" (as quoted in "The Great Liberal Death Wish," *Imprimis,* May 1979, Hillsdale College, Michigan).

An abundance, therefore, is present in the "other books" of scripture which have come through the "choice seer." Highly capsulized in the case of the less essential, and highly pointed in the case of the salvational truths, this material is all highly prized by the serious disciple.

All of it was brought forth through a "choice seer" by the power and the love of God. But we must not be diverted from the "what" and "why" of its substance by unproductive stirrings over the yet-to-be-fully-revealed "how" of its coming forth. As to the details of the process he used, Joseph said that it was not intended for the world to know all the particulars[4] (see *History of the Church* 1:220).

The Book of Mormon possesses a special "convincing" power, whether for Jews, for Gentiles, or for the seed of Lehi.

Obviously, this "convincing" power, borne by the witnessing Spirit of God, provides assurances in the most demonstrative and persuasive ways. How precious, indeed, these "other books" really are! With their lode of truth and simple but deep doctrine at their cores, they indeed carry their own witness of their authenticity and also provide "convincing" power in support of the Bible (see 2 Nephi 3:11).

Some other attesting and interesting insights are emerging which are less at the core of these "other books" and more in the supporting penumbra. For the thoughtful believer, these will further enhance appreciation for these scriptures, particularly the priceless Book of Mormon. But with reference to this mortal existence, belief in the truthfulness of the Book of Mormon will not be removed entirely from the realm of faith. Though various supporting evidences will continue to emerge that further attest to the prophetic mission of the Prophet Joseph Smith and to what a rich, remarkable, and resplendent record the Book of Mormon is, convictions concerning its core message will still require faith and study.

Believers will be patient during such further unfolding. They will note that all the scriptures remain, for now, in the realm of faith, including the Bible. One can establish the authenticity and historicity of a Pauline epistle, for example, and still refuse to accept the validity of its witness of Christ or to heed its teachings regarding the reality of the resurrection. Hence we can be assured that enough plausible, supporting data and external evidence will come forth to prevent scoffers from having a field day with the scriptures, but not enough to remove the requirement of faith.

This has implications for the faithful who wish to obtain more of the word of the Lord. Their doing so will in no way depend upon supporting evidence man may discover. It will depend in large measure upon their full acceptance of and serious application to that which has already been given. This is a declared and deliberate test of faith: "And when they shall have received this, which is expedient that they should have first, to try their faith, and if it shall so be that they shall believe these things then shall the greater things be made manifest unto them. . . . Behold, I was about to write them, all which were engraven upon the plates of

Nephi, but the Lord forbade it, saying: I will try the faith of my people." (3 Nephi 26:9, 11.)

Writers and editors of the Book of Mormon repeatedly stressed their selectivity in both their recording and their choosing—under the inspiration of heaven—what was to be finally included in that superb volume. This assured that, with the restoration of "plain and precious things," those who "despise" plainness would be without excuse. Like certain earlier counterparts, they would be delivered over to stumbling of their own making (see Jacob 4:14–15).

Naturally, some would like to have even more contextual material about the life, times, and culture of the peoples in the Book of Mormon. In fact, though, there is much more already given in the book than most of us have been able to assimilate and appreciate thus far. Nevertheless, such supportive but ancillary data are not the purpose for which the book has been brought forward. This reality is stated very early in the book itself: "Wherefore, the things which are pleasing unto the world I do not write, but the things which are pleasing unto God and unto those who are not of the world" (1 Nephi 6:5).

No wonder these scriptures fail to please or to impress the world. There are those who prefer details on ancient agriculture to the "bread of life," who prefer information on the rising of dynasties to insights on the rising of Jesus from the tomb. Perhaps this is so because the former type of data is very interesting without being very demanding. The second type demands both faith and, thereafter, a certain behavior.

The Book of Mormon contains disclosing candor concerning author anxiety about selectivity: "Nevertheless, I do not write anything upon plates save it be that I think it be sacred. And now, if I do err, even did they err of old; not that I would excuse myself because of other men, but because of the weakness which is in me, according to the flesh, I would excuse myself." (1 Nephi 19:6.)

Nephi later added another caveat: "And I engraved that which is pleasing unto God. And if my people are pleased with the things of God they will be pleased with mine engravings which are upon these plates." (2 Nephi 5:32.)

Thus the procedure by which the book emerged, concerning which Joseph testified from jail, was anything but random and its message is anything but casual: "And now I, Moroni, have written the words which were commanded me, according to my memory; and I have told you the things which I have sealed up; therefore touch them not in order that ye may translate; for that thing is forbidden you, except by and by it shall be wisdom in God" (Ether 5:1).

In any case, the other Nephite records, still sealed, remain unbequeathed and untranslated. The translated, small plates of Nephi contained the religious rather than the secular history. The sealed portion yet to come forth will be very valuable. (3 Nephi 26:10–11.) In fact, this sweeping portion will contain "a revelation from God, from the beginning of the world to the ending thereof" (2 Nephi 27:7, 10–11). Such a cumulative record yet to be revealed is something to be awaited with "anxious expectation" in that "time to come in the which nothing shall be withheld," as the Prophet Joseph was promised in the prison-temple (D&C 121:27–28).

The larger plates of Nephi appear focused on "the more particular part of the history" of the Lord's people. Better a few more verses concerning the reality of the resurrection than a few more concerning kingly succession. Therefore, as in John's gospel (see John 21:25; 20:30–31), we do not have a "hundredth part of the proceedings of this people," but we have the things of most worth (Jacob 3:13).

The chief editor, Mormon, who worked and searched his way through much amassed material, was especially pleased with the many references to Christ included in the small plates of Nephi. The deep, anticipatory Christology (fifth and sixth centuries B.C.) fascinated Mormon (in the fourth century of the Christian era) nearly a thousand years later! Mormon added his editorial comment about the Messianic richness particularly of Nephi's and Jacob's teachings: "The things which are upon these plates pleasing me, because of the prophecies of the coming of Christ . . ." (Words of Mormon 1:4).

Mormon expressed the hope that his son, Moroni, would have a later opportunity not to expand further on the endless military campaigns but to "write somewhat" more "concerning Christ" (Words of Mormon 1:2). Alas, a lonely Moroni instead found himself in this circumstance: "Behold, my father hath made this record, and he hath written the intent thereof. And behold, I would write it also if I had room upon the plates, but I have not; and ore I have none, for I am alone. My father hath been slain in battle, and all my kinsfolk, and I have not friends nor whither to go; and how long the Lord will suffer that I may live I know not." (Mormon 8:5.)

All this and so much more preceded the gifted translation by a "choice seer."

Little wonder that, whether in Liberty Jail or Philadelphia, Joseph Smith wanted the world to know "the Book of Mormon is true." Sad to say, what Joseph so remarkably translated is, by some, even now taken "lightly." We can scarcely regard Joseph Smith as a "choice seer" if we do not savor the choice scripture which came through him. In contrast, when ancient Joseph saw in vision the scattering and driving of his posterity, he "wept"; however, when he saw Joseph Smith, Jr., the means by which his descendants would be "brought back to the true fold," his "heart rejoiced and his soul was satisfied." (Father's Blessing, 1834.)

It now remains for Church members to partake more fully of these "other books" than we have done in the past. As we do so, our hearts will "rejoice," and our souls too will be "satisfied."

On March 20, 1839, in Liberty Jail, Joseph received the revelation now known as section 121. The same day he wrote to the members of the Church, bearing testimony that "the Book of Mormon is true . . . the Book of Covenants is true" (*Writings*, p. 407). Doubtless Joseph was then very anxious that, even as further revelation flowed from the Lord, Church members appreciate what had already been given through him.

Notes

1. This is not to say, of course, that Joseph had not earlier been clear and declarative regarding the Book of Mormon: for instance, in an 1834 sermon he observed, "Take away the Book of Mormon and the revelations, and where is

our religion?" (*Teachings*, p. 71). In 1835 the Prophet used a parable to describe the book and how "a man took and hid [it] in his field, securing it by his faith, to spring up in the last days" (*Teachings*, p. 98).

2. "Establish" denotes "to put beyond doubt; to settle, to make firm and stable." In illustration, Alma spoke "to establish the words of Amulek," his colleague. What Alma said involved both confirmation and elaboration of Amulek's testifying and warning words to Zeezrom. (See Alma 12:1.) Besides establishing biblical truth, because of the Book of Mormon's ties to the law of Moses it may come to be appreciated more highly now as also being something of a window through which to view pre-exilic Israel.

3. The Lord's prophets may not always initially comprehend the full significance of the words that come through them from the Lord. Elder Orson Pratt surmised that Joseph Smith did not appear to have been aware of different time zones affecting the time of day when Christ was taken down from the cross —mid-afternoon in Jerusalem and "in the morning" in the Americas. (See Matthew 27:45–50; 3 Nephi 10:9; *Journal of Discourses* 15:260.)

4. Joseph's hesitation to speak in detail about the translation process is reflected in his response to his brother Hyrum's request at a conference held in Orange, Ohio, in October 1831 that Joseph provide a first-hand account concerning the coming forth of the Book of Mormon. The Prophet replied that "it was not intended to tell the world all the particulars of the coming forth of the Book of Mormon and . . . it was not expedient for him to relate these things." (Stephen D. Ricks, "Joseph Smith's Means and Methods of Translating the Book of Mormon." *Preliminary Report*, F.A.R.M.S. R.I.C.-84, p. 1.)

CHAPTER 3

"Shall Grow Together" 2 Nephi 3:12

As already noted, the prison-temple provided time for the Prophet Joseph to express himself in ways which reflected the converging of his learning and the growing together of his insights and experiences. His communications from Liberty Jail included not only his testimony as to the "other books" of scripture but also reflected his capacity to see the relevance of numerous biblical passages (see chapter 1). However, Joseph's busy ministry did not provide him with the time and opportunities to effect a full, articulate convergence of the Bible with all the scripture which had come through him as a "choice seer."

Without Joseph's revelatory role the promise that the writings of ancient prophets on different hemispheres "shall grow together" (2 Nephi 3:12) simply could not have been fulfilled. Granted, the converging process was to come to a more full fruition after Joseph's day. But Joseph, the "choice seer," translated the Book of Mormon, received other revelations, testified as to the truthfulness of these scriptures, and sealed his testimony with his martyr's blood. For us in the modern Church it is imperative more than ever before that these various books become *one* in our hands, hearts, and heads.

It is clear that Joseph Smith's testimony about the truthfulness of the Bible, the Book of Mormon, and the Doctrine and Covenants, given in his extremity of the Liberty Jail experience, reflected not only his awareness of the shared purposes of these books and their converging relevance but also his sense of urgency about that culminating unity.

Given the divine design of the "other books," believers in and students of them regard the correlative relationships between ancient and modern scriptures as unsurprising. They are the expected latticework of the Lord, and the multiple interweavings and abundant cross-supports among them are part of a natural pattern for scriptures that were to converge doctrinally and "grow together."

These correlated interweavings should give pause even to near-believers. Of course, for those for whom any explanation of the origins of latter-day scripture will do except the real one, there is no remedy.

> And in fine, wo unto all those who tremble, and are angry because of the truth of God! For behold, he that is built upon the rock receiveth it with gladness; and he that is built upon a sandy foundation trembleth lest he shall fall.
>
> Wo be unto him that shall say: We have received the word of God, and we need no more of the word of God, for we have enough! (2 Nephi 28:28–29.)

Some are genuinely and understandably interested in the facts and processes of the Restoration. Disbelievers, however, are intensely anxious to try to establish any alternative that disputes the divinity in the process. For them it is really not that any explanation but one *will do*—for them, one explanation definitely *will not do!*

This preoccupation with process ignores the emerging substance of the Restoration. For instance, after all the flurry about accompanying history, there stands the Book of Mormon, waiting to be reckoned with. Perhaps anxiety over the neglect accorded the book prompted the Prophet's testimony from Liberty Jail. Ever to be remembered is the fact that while the Book of Mormon was translated by Joseph, it was *not* his book. It was from God, said Joseph, that "we received the Book of Mormon" (*Writings*, p. 399). Twice in the same epistle he urged his testimony of the Book of Mormon upon Church members.

In majestic simplicity the Lord declared his correlated pattern of witnessing communication: "I speak the same words unto one nation like unto another. And when the two nations shall run together the testimony of the two nations shall run together also." (2 Nephi 29:8.) Thus the words of Ezekiel are correlated fully with the words of Nephi regarding the oneness of purpose of these modern and ancient records (see Ezekiel 37:19; 1 Nephi 13:40–41).

Notwithstanding modern printing and binding formats of our standard works, then, the growing together has reference not to paper and pages but to the key doctrines in all the books of scripture. For example, the following scriptures concerning the nature of petitionary prayer, when clustered together, provide so much more critically needed candlepower than when considered apart:

> And all things, whatsoever ye shall ask in prayer, believing, ye shall receive (Matthew 21:22).

> Ye ask, and receive not, because ye ask amiss, that ye may consume it upon your lusts (James 4:3).

> Yea, I know that God will give liberally to him that asketh. Yea, my God will give me, if I ask not amiss. (2 Nephi 4:35.)

> And whatsoever ye shall ask the Father in my name, which is right, believing that ye shall receive, behold it shall be given unto you (3 Nephi 18:20).

> And now, if God, who has created you, on whom you are dependent for your lives and for all that ye have and are, doth grant unto you whatsoever ye ask that is right, in faith, believing that ye shall receive, O then, how ye ought to impart of the substance that ye have one to another (Mosiah 4:21).

> Likewise the Spirit also helpeth our infirmities: for we know not what we should pray for as we ought: but the Spirit itself maketh intercession for us with groanings which cannot be uttered (Romans 8:26).

> He that asketh in the Spirit asketh according to the will of God; wherefore it is done even as he asketh (D&C 46:30).

Prayer is petitioning, but it also involves tutoring. Imprisoned Joseph pleaded with God, "Let thine anger be kindled against our enemies" (D&C 121:5). But God counseled patience and said, in effect, "not yet"; he had "in reserve a swift judgment in the season thereof" (see D&C 121:12, 15, 24).

Such spiritual truths, so many of which have come to us through "a choice seer," are especially impressive in their elaboration and correlation. The coaching of the Prophet Joseph by a loving Lord is nowhere more tender than that which we witness in the prison-temple.

Yet we must not neglect to observe that so much of the seer's work was accomplished at the front end of the Restoration, including the laying down of many doctrines through revelation and translation. The doctrinal density of the Book of Mormon, for instance, clearly overshadows the portion devoted to history or to such details as the description of Nephite weights and measures (see Alma 11:3–19).

The book's structure, then, obviously and intentionally is secondary to its substance, and its historical plot to its principles. The Book of Mormon's innumerable insights in matters spiritual and its rich and resplendent doctrinal declarations constitute their own witness.

Clearly, this book came *through* a "choice seer"—Joseph Smith—but not *from* that seer. Some, desperate for an alternative explanation, almost seem to suppose Joseph was getting help from some theological mail-order supply house.

To the human mind it is amazing that such rich revelations and translations should come through an untrained individual such as Joseph was. The reason, of course, is that, though Joseph did not spell perfectly, he came to know the grammar of the gospel, because he was God's apt pupil.

The following scriptures tell us something about "why" God has usually determined to rely upon those of lower worldly estate, such as Joseph Smith, to do his work, upon the very type of individual whom establishments can imprison in Rome or Missouri.

> For ye see . . . how that not many wise men after the flesh, not many mighty, not many noble, are called:
> But God hath chosen the foolish things of the world to confound the wise; . . . the weak things of the world to confound the things which are mighty. (1 Corinthians 1:26–27.)

> Wherefore, I the Lord, . . . called upon my servant Joseph Smith, Jun., and spake unto him from heaven, and gave him commandments; . . .
>
> The weak things of the world shall come forth and break down the mighty and strong ones, . . .
>
> That the fulness of my gospel might be proclaimed by the weak and the simple unto the ends of the world, . . .
>
> Behold, . . . these commandments . . . were given unto my servants in their weakness. (D&C 1:17, 19, 23, 24.)

> And I have sent forth the fulness of my gospel by . . . Joseph; and in weakness have I blessed him (D&C 35:17).

> Verily, thus saith the Lord unto you, my servant Joseph Smith, . . . for unto this end have I raised you up, that I might show forth my wisdom through the weak things of the earth (D&C 124:1).

Joseph's "weaknesses" included what the world would call inadequacies—in literary and grammatical skills, for example. But the Book of Mormon itself propounds the encouraging doctrine that for those who humble themselves before God, he will make their weaknesses strengths (see 2 Nephi 3:13; Ether 12:27, 37). Nowhere is this transformation better exemplified than in the translation of the Book of Mormon, in which, because of Joseph's "weakness," both the process and the substance were directed of the Savior. Some of Nephi's concluding words reflect the appropriateness of this direction:

> And now, my beloved brethren, and also Jew, and all ye ends of the earth, hearken unto these words and believe in Christ; and if ye believe not in these words believe in Christ. And if ye shall believe in Christ ye will believe in these words, for they are the words of Christ, and he hath given them unto me. (2 Nephi 33:10.)

The book's witnessing words will even figure, quite confrontationally, in the drama of the final and just judgment: "And if they are not the words of Christ, judge ye—for Christ will show unto you, with power and great glory, that they are his words, at the last day; and you and I shall stand face to face before his bar; and ye shall know that I have been commanded of him to write these things, notwithstanding my weakness" (2 Nephi 33:11).

Joseph Smith, who received so many such words, had this to say about the persuasive power of the words of Jesus: "Every word that proceedeth from the mouth of Jehovah has such an influence over the human mind—the logical mind—that it is convincing without other testimony. Faith cometh by hearing." (*Words*, p. 237.)

The growing together of scriptures is not new, of course. Did not the New Testament Jesus declare, in yet another powerful example of convergence, that the "Old Testament" scriptures testified of him? "Search the scriptures; . . . and they are they which testify of me" (John 5:39).

Jesus similarly invoked the reminding power of symbolism as he sought to stir his disbelieving audiences in this same regard: "And as Moses lifted up the serpent in the wilderness, even so must the Son of man be lifted up: that whosoever believeth in him should not perish, but have eternal life." (John 3:14–15. See also Numbers 21:5–9; Helaman 8:14–15.)

With such splendid ties between Moses and Jesus, should the "cast" on the Mount of Transfiguration be any surprise? "And, behold, there appeared unto them Moses and Elias talking with him" (Matthew 17:3).

Given the importance of such longitudinal ties, it should not surprise us that the foretelling role of the law of Moses is made more clear in the plain and precious Book of Mormon:

> Yet the Lord God saw that his people were a stiffnecked people, and he appointed unto them a law, even the law of Moses.
>
> And many signs, and wonders, and types, and shadows showed he unto them, concerning his coming; and also holy prophets spake unto them concerning his coming; and yet they hardened their hearts, and understood not that the law of Moses availeth nothing except it were through the atonement of his blood. (Mosiah 3:14–15.)

What came later through Joseph Smith, came earlier through John:

> For had ye believed Moses, ye would have believed me: for he wrote of me (John 5:46).
>
> And now, Moses, my son, I will speak unto thee concerning this earth upon which thou standest; and thou shalt write the things which I shall speak.
>
> And in a day when the children of men shall esteem my words as naught and take many of them from the book which thou shalt write, behold, I will raise up another like unto thee; and they shall

be had again among the children of men—among as many as shall believe. (Moses 1:40–41.)

In fact, even the timing of the Book of Mormon's latter-day emergence reflected divine design; it came in response to the growing human need for reassuring and witnessing words regarding the Savior. It came for an age when far too many are disturbed about the historicity of Christ. The sparse mentionings of Jesus in secular history are spectacularly offset by the flood of scriptural witness of him that came through the latter-day seer in a unique process.

Moroni, so much of whose life was involved with the preparation, preservation, and coming forth of the Book of Mormon, declared that the whole process of the book's coming forth "shall be done by the power of God" (Mormon 8:16). He reiterated this theme in the line now published in what is probably his contribution to the title page: ". . . to come forth in . . . the interpretation thereof by the gift and power of God."

Whatever the combination of individual prophets—Enoch, Moses, Isaiah, Nephi, Alma, Paul, Moroni, or Joseph—the links between them and the growing together of the scriptures they produced are clear. Each separate strand of prophetic utterance, though interwoven into a pattern of divine design, can be followed back to a single Source, a loving, redemptive Father whose central and grand declared purpose is to bring to pass the immortality and eternal life of man (see Moses 1:39). Hence, the Lord "formed the earth and made it . . . to be inhabited" (Isaiah 45:18). As told to Joseph in jail, such plans were made anciently in the grand "Council of the Eternal God" before this world was (D&C 121:30–32).

The testifying and integrating role of the "other books," as they "grow together," should not be underestimated. The convergence, however, is not merely to demonstrate correlative cleverness but to provide saving truths, such as that Jesus of Nazareth is the very Christ, whose redemptive atonement is at the center of the Father's plan for mankind.

Though other names (Messiah, Son of God, the Lamb, etc.) are used, from the outset, the Book of Mormon, through Jacob, foretells of Christ, *by name*, commencing with 2 Nephi 10:3 (even

the name of His mother, Mary), well before his birth (see also
Mosiah 3:8; Alma 7:10).

The Book of Mormon emphatically declares that the law of
Moses was purposefully to point the Jewish people and the world
to the birth and coming of the Messiah, Jesus. The Old Testament as we have received it is silent with regard to the specific
name of the Savior to come; however, it lists many of his special
and sacred titles and sets forth numerous prophecies pertaining
to his birth, mortal ministry, crucifixion, and atonement. Moreover, despite the lack of this information in our Old Testament as
we have received it, the Book of Mormon prophet Jacob, writing
in the fifth or sixth century B.C., stated that "none of the [earlier]
prophets have written, nor prophesied, save they have spoken
concerning this Christ" (Jacob 7:11).

Also, when the Old Testament uses the term *anointed* to refer
to "the Anointed One," the Greek translation would be *Christos*
(see footnote for 1 Samuel 2:10, LDS edition of the King James
version of the Bible).

Perhaps some biblical scriptures regarding the Savior were
editorially subdued. For instance, one wonders whether Zechariah received authority from the Lord to say *only* these next
words regarding a special moment associated with Jesus' second
coming: "And one shall say unto him, What are these wounds in
thine hands? Then he shall answer, Those with which I was
wounded in the house of my friends." (Zechariah 13:6.)

Or did Zechariah say more which, alas, ended up being
among the untransmitted "plain and precious things" "held
back"? Either way, latter-day scriptural references are strikingly
clear concerning this event:

> And then shall the Jews look upon me and say: What are these
> wounds in thine hands and in thy feet?
> Then shall they know that I am the Lord; for I will say unto
> them: These wounds are the wounds with which I was wounded in
> the house of my friends. I am he who was lifted up. I am Jesus that
> was crucified. I am the Son of God.
> And then shall they weep because of their iniquities; then shall
> they lament because they persecuted their king. (D&C 45:51–53.)

Jesus' declarations as to his remarkable premortal role and his feelings carried over as the Jehovah of the Old Testament were clearly given during his mortal ministry:

> Jesus said unto them, Verily, verily, I say unto you, Before Abraham was, I am (John 8:58).

> O Jerusalem, Jerusalem, thou that killest the prophets, and stonest them which are sent unto thee, how often would I have gathered thy children together, even as a hen gathereth her chickens under her wings, and ye would not! (Matthew 23:37.)

Paul was not confused about whom Moses chose: "By faith Moses, when he was come to years, refused to be called the son of Pharaoh's daughter; choosing rather to suffer affliction with the people of God, than to enjoy the pleasures of sin for a season; esteeming the reproach of Christ greater riches than the treasures in Egypt: for he had respect unto the recompense of the reward" (Hebrews 11:24–26).

Now, in a time when scrolls have been found in Qumran, writings at Nag Hammadi, and tablets at Ebla, we must at least consider the probability that other ancient but lost documents and lost scriptures may contain further striking and Christ-centered things. Among those writings lost are the writings of Samuel, the seer; Nathan; the Acts of Solomon; Shemaiah; Ahijah; Iddo; Jehu; and Enoch. Joshua mentions the book of Jasher (Joshua 10:13). To these must be added whatever else was "kept back" from ever reaching the dedicated translators of the Bible (see 1 Nephi 13:32, 34, 40).

In turn, the Book of Mormon alerts us to the book of Zenos (Jacob 5) and still other missing books: "And behold, also Zenock, and also Ezias, and also Isaiah, and Jeremiah, (Jeremiah being that same prophet who testified of the destruction of Jerusalem) and now we know that Jerusalem was destroyed according to the words of Jeremiah. O then why not the Son of God come, according to his prophecy?" (Helaman 8:20.)

Would these "books," if found, contain some of the precious references to Jesus, even by name? We do not now know. We know, however, that there are more records than we now possess: "And a book of remembrance was kept, in the which was recorded, in the language of Adam, for it was given unto as many as called upon God to write by the spirit of inspiration" (Moses 6:5).

The absence of scriptural records which have been lost does make a difference. By way of example, Matthew mentions a prophecy we do not now have about Jesus' being known as a Nazarene.

> And he came and dwelt in a city called Nazareth: that it might be fulfilled which was spoken by the prophets, He shall be called a Nazarene (Matthew 2:23).

While the scriptures make clear that Jesus was to be born in Bethlehem (Micah 5:2), he was also to be a Nazarene in view of the place where he would grow up. This particular misunderstanding proved to be a genuine stumbling point for some, especially the Jewish scribes and the illuminati of the time: "Others said, This is the Christ. But some said, Shall Christ come out of Galilee? Hath not the scripture said, That Christ cometh of the seed of David, and out of the town of Bethlehem, where David was?" (John 7:41–42.)

We also know that some things are omitted from scripture as a function of sheer voluminosity:

> And there are also many other things which Jesus did, the which, if they should be written every one, I suppose that even the world itself could not contain the books that should be written. Amen. (John 21:25.)

> And there had many things transpired which, in the eyes of some, would be great and marvelous; nevertheless, they cannot all be written in this book; yea, this book cannot contain even a hundredth part of what was done among so many people in the space of twenty and five years (3 Nephi 5:8).

Other omissions occur for other causes. The Lord may have withheld certain specifics from certain people as an act of mercy, so far as their accountability is concerned.

Could there also have been a deliberate, divine withholding in this matter of the mortal name of the Messiah? Purposeful withholding has occurred before.

> And when they shall have received this, which is expedient that they should have first, *to try their faith,* and *if* it shall so be that they shall *believe* these things *then* shall the *greater things* be *made manifest* unto them. . . .

Behold, I was about to write them, all which were engraven upon the plates of Nephi, but the Lord forbade it, saying: I will try the faith of my people. . . .

Behold, it came to pass on the morrow that the multitude gathered themselves together, and they both saw and heard these children; yea, even babes did open their mouths and utter marvelous things; and the things which they did utter were forbidden that there should not any man write them. (3 Nephi 26:9, 11, 16; italics added.)

Whatever the cause for the Old Testament's silence regarding Christ's name, we have clear and early references in the Book of Mormon on that matter. As the following selections illustrate, the earliest occurred between 559 and 545 B.C., *after* the Nephites had reached the western hemisphere:

Behold, my soul delighteth in proving unto my people the truth of the coming of Christ; for, for this end hath the law of Moses been given; and all things which have been given of God from the beginning of the world, unto man, are the typifying of him (2 Nephi 11:4).

And, notwithstanding we believe in Christ, we keep the law of Moses, and look forward with steadfastness unto Christ, until the law shall be fulfilled (2 Nephi 25:24).

And we talk of Christ, we rejoice in Christ, we preach of Christ, we prophesy of Christ, and we write according to our prophecies, that our children may know to what source they may look for a remission of their sins (2 Nephi 25:26).

For, for this intent have we written these things, that they may know that we knew of Christ, and we had a hope of his glory many hundred years before his coming; and not only we ourselves had a hope of his glory, but also all the holy prophets which were before us.

Behold, they believed in Christ and worshiped the Father in his name, and also we worship the Father in his name. And for this intent we keep the law of Moses, it pointing our souls to him; and for this cause it is sanctified unto us for righteousness, even as it was accounted unto Abraham in the wilderness to be obedient unto the commands of God in offering up his son Isaac, which is a similitude of God and his Only Begotten Son. (Jacob 4:4–5.)

In the book of Moses, which probably was written 3,500 years ago and contains revealed information covering the period from Adam to Noah, the special name is given several times.

Whether pertaining to the law of Moses or to God's creations, clearly this is a witnessing world for all who have eyes to see.

> And behold, this is the whole meaning of the law, every whit pointing to that great and last sacrifice; and that great and last sacrifice will be the Son of God, yea, infinite and eternal (Alma 34:14).

> Behold, my soul delighteth in proving unto my people the truth of the coming of Christ; for, for this end hath the law of Moses been given; and all things which have been given of God from the beginning of the world, unto man, are the typifying of him (2 Nephi 11:4).

> And behold, all things have their likeness, and all things are created and made to bear record of me, both things which are temporal, and things which are spiritual; things which are in the heavens above, and things which are on the earth, and things which are in the earth, and things which are under the earth, both above and beneath: all things bear record of me (Moses 6:63).

These and numerous other converging references affirm that the law of Moses was intended to point mortals to Jesus Christ. In fact, as scholars are now exploring, the keeping of the law of Moses by groups included in the accounts of the Book of Mormon will yet prove to be another evidence of that book's divine origins and coming forth. Thus many things are growing together.

Verses and words we might previously have passed over lightly and uncomprehendingly are now coming to be appreciated as laden with significance. One example is 2 Nephi 11:4, quoted above. This and a statement in Alma underscore the understated Mosaic and pre-exilic roots of the Book of Mormon.

> Yea, and the people did observe to keep the commandments of the Lord; and they were strict in observing the ordinances of God, according to the law of Moses; for they were taught to keep the law of Moses until it should be fulfilled (Alma 30:3).

Most of us have sped by such verses without realizing their implications. In the timing of the Lord, the need is now arriving for us to see more clearly the significance and implications of such verses. Filled with faith and scholarship, some—such as Jack Welch and his colleagues at Brigham Young University— are bringing afresh such possibilities to our attention, as have Hugh Nibley and others earlier on.

Inattentiveness to spiritual things is not confined to our time. So many who were "looking beyond the mark" missed all the indicators of Jesus' mortal Messiahship, including the foretelling law of Moses:

> But behold, the Jews were a stiffnecked people; and they despised the words of plainness, and killed the prophets, and sought for things that they could not understand. Wherefore, because of their blindness, which blindness came by looking beyond the mark, they must needs fall; for God hath taken away his plainness from them, and delivered unto them many things which they cannot understand, because they desired it. And because they desired it God hath done it, that they may stumble. (Jacob 4:14.)

The Old Testament prophecies pertaining to the coming, atoning, and crucifying of a redeeming Messiah are both glorious and numerous. The following sampling may suffice. But observe that, at the time, the ability to discern the significance of these scriptures would have required a mind attuned and eyes willing to see.

> I shall see him, but not now: I shall behold him, but not nigh: there shall come a Star out of Jacob, and a Sceptre shall rise out of Israel, and shall smite the corners of Moab, and destroy all the children of Sheth (Numbers 24:17).

> The Lord thy God will raise up unto thee a Prophet from the midst of thee, of thy brethren, like unto me; unto him ye shall hearken (Deuteronomy 18:15).

> I will declare the decree: the Lord hath said unto me, Thou art my Son; this day have I begotten thee (Psalm 2:7).

> My God, my God, why hast thou forsaken me? why art thou so far from helping me, and from the words of my roaring? (Psalm 22:1.)

> For dogs have compassed me: the assembly of the wicked have inclosed me: they pierced my hands and my feet (Psalm 22:16).

> He keepeth all his bones: not one of them is broken (Psalm 34:20).

> They gave me also gall for my meat; and in my thirst they gave me vinegar to drink (Psalm 69:21).

> The Lord hath sworn, and will not repent, Thou art a priest for ever after the order of Melchizedek (Psalm 110:4).

Jesus, in his mortal Messiahship, even cited certain of these foretelling verses, but to little avail for the hard-hearted and hard-headed:

> The stone which the builders refused is become the head stone of the corner (Psalm 118:22).

> Jesus saith unto them, Did ye never read in the scriptures, The stone which the builders rejected, the same is become the head of the corner: this is the Lord's doing, and it is marvelous in our eyes? (Matthew 21:42.)

> And as Moses lifted up the serpent in the wilderness, even so must the Son of man be lifted up:
> That whosoever believeth in him should not perish, but have eternal life. (John 3:14–15.) (See also 2 Nephi 25:20; Numbers 21:5–9.)

A synonym of the Savior was foretold in one verse: "Therefore the Lord himself shall give you a sign; Behold, a virgin shall conceive, and bear a son, and shall call his name Immanuel" (Isaiah 7:14).

Were Old Testament prophets restrained from being more specific with regard to Jesus, his name, and his role? Or were they more specific than surviving records now indicate? Or was the writing of such specifics reserved for those other than Old Testament prophets? Has something been lost in the transmittal? Has something been lost in biblical translation?

While Jesus declared that the scriptures "testify" of him (John 5:39), he neither expected nor received much coverage in secular history. Therefore it is no surprise for studious Christians to learn that secular history is nearly silent about the ministry of Jesus. Three writers only, so far as we know, each born after Jesus' death, touched slightly upon the historicity of Christ. Tacitus (about A.D. 55–117), the greatest Roman historian, wrote only this of Jesus: "Christus . . . had undergone the death penalty in the reign of Tiberius, by sentence of the procurator Pontius Pilatus" (*Annals of Tacitus*, Book XV, p. 283).

Suetonius (about A.D. 70–140), a Roman who wrote about the lives of the Caesars, called Jesus "Chrestus" and provided a sentence linking Chrestus to civil disturbance; yet even this may contain a possible chronological error (Suetonius, *Lives of the Caesars*, Book V, pp. 52, 53).

Josephus (about A.D. 37–95), in his *Antiquities,* wrote briefly of the founder of Christianity, but possible interpolations and omissions cloud his meager lines. He also wrote briefly of the murder of "a good man," John the Baptist, because of Herod's political alarm, and also of James, described as the "brother of one said to be Christ."

How little we would know about Jesus if we relied solely on secular history without the blessed Holy Bible!

Who was the Pharaoh of the Exodus, for instance? Perhaps Ramses II, but available secular history oddly does not record the miraculous exodus of a large number of Hebrew slaves defying and leaving their Egyptian masters.

To Jesus' comment about a prophet's having no honor in his own country and in his own household (see Matthew 13:57) might therefore be added "in his own time."

But when He comes again . . . !

Meanwhile, having additional witnesses of Jesus' Saviorhood is vital. So is having additional witnesses to the Father's plan of salvation, especially since all that divinity does is, in fact, focused "for the benefit of the world" (2 Nephi 26:24). Has not the Psalmist said, "We are the people of his pasture, and the sheep of his hand"? (Psalm 95:7.) God has no distracting hobbies. One's eye is to be single to his glory—and his glory, happily, is to bring to pass the immortality and eternal life of man.

Moreover, embedded in the world around us, as well as in God's word, are so many things which point to Christ (see, for example, 2 Nephi 11:4, quoted earlier in this chapter). In fact, it is a witnessing universe. For those who have eyes to see, "all things bear record of [Christ]" (Moses 6:63).

> But Alma said unto him: Thou hast had signs enough; will ye tempt your God? Will ye say, Show unto me a sign, when ye have the testimony of all these thy brethren, and also all the holy prophets? The scriptures are laid before thee, yea, and all things denote there is a God; yea, even the earth, and all things that are upon the face of it, yea, and its motion, yea, and also all the planets which move in their regular form do witness that there is a Supreme Creator. (Alma 30:44.)

How essential for faith in our time is the growing together of all witnessing scriptures! How understandable the urgency of

Joseph's testimony in Liberty Jail concerning the significance of all the scriptures! For Joseph to verify from jail the truth of Jesus' existence was not casual or superficial testimony, since Joseph had been an "eyewitness" of Jesus on more than one special occasion before the days in Liberty Jail.

The faithful who, through these "other books," possess such a treasure trove of truth—almost all of which came through the Prophet Joseph—have a basic challenge. Our challenge is not simply to shelve them but to delve into them, not alone to possess them, but to witness of them! A fundamental challenge was well described by Austin Farrer, who wrote of the need for articulate Christians: "Though argument does not create conviction, lack of it destroys belief. What seems to be proved may not be embraced; but what no one shows the ability to defend is quickly abandoned. Rational argument does not create belief, but it maintains a climate in which belief may flourish." (Austin Farrer, *Light on C. S. Lewis,* Jocelyn Gibb, ed. [New York: Harcourt, Brace and World, Inc., 1966], p. 26.)

We can and should be articulate believers. We can and should so proclaim, testify, and teach, readily and humbly, concerning these added books of scripture. Meanwhile, at the same time, we should honor and use the Holy Bible. Joseph Smith did both; apparently it never occurred to him to do otherwise.

It is not amiss, either, to observe how the growing together of scriptures facilitates another kind of growing, for the revelations received in Liberty Jail are perhaps as explanatory and deliberately tutorial as any ever received and recorded!

Out of this growing together there is developing among faithful Latter-day Saint scholars and other Church members an increased appreciation as to how rich these "other books" are—beyond the capacity of Joseph Smith or anyone else unaided by the Lord to produce.

The remarkable process of translation occurred through a bright but largely unschooled young man. Unlettered Joseph, for instance, reportedly didn't know there was a wall around Jerusalem until he encountered and puzzled over that reality in the early work of translating from the plates. Emma verified for Joseph the fact that there was a wall around Jerusalem. (*History of the Reorganized Church of Jesus Christ of Latter Day Saints,* 4:44.)

When, for a brief period, Emma was his scribe, Joseph would "dictate" to her. When they were interrupted for one reason or another and resumed translating, Joseph "would begin at once where he had left off, without either seeing the manuscript or having any portion of it read to him" ("Last Testimony," *The Saints' Advocate*, October 1879, p. 52). In contrast, those of us who dictate often will usually ask our secretaries, after interruptions, "Now, where was I?"

Parley P. Pratt was present in May 1831 when Joseph Smith received the revelation that is now section 50 of the Doctrine and Covenants. He recorded:

> After we had joined in prayer in [Joseph Smith's] translating room, he dictated in our presence the following revelation: — (Each sentence was uttered slowly and very distinctly, and with a pause between each, sufficiently long for it to be recorded, by an ordinary writer, in long hand.)
>
> This was the manner in which all his written revelations were dictated and written. There was never any hesitation, reviewing, or reading back, in order to keep the run of the subject; neither did any of these communications undergo revisions, interlinings, or corrections. As he dictated them so they stood, so far as I have witnessed; and I was present to witness the dictation of several communications of several pages each. (*Autobiography of Parley P. Pratt* [Deseret Book Co., 1972], p. 62.)

The processes of revelation and translation varied. Though not described with clinical detail and consistency, they were constant in reflecting the gifts and the power of God. Whether in Joseph's translating from ancient records, or in his receiving and recording certain direct revelations, or in his rewording portions of the Bible under inspiration, the Lord clearly oversaw the vital process.

Concerning the process of translation or receiving revelation, then, would the world accept such a process, even if all the facts were known, while rejecting its result?

So it was that the remarkable work of translating the Book of Mormon was accomplished, as Joseph Smith said: "Through the medium of the Urim and Thummim I translated the record by the gift and power of God" (*Times and Seasons*, vol. 3 [1842], p. 707).

What the "choice seer" translated is laden with significance. The work of several years by anthropologist John Sorenson of

BYU and others in demonstrating more about possible "host" circumstances in ancient Meso-America is interesting. What is there described as plausible may not prove finally persuasive, but it creates a climate in which the interest can be quickened, as the portrait of a special people emerges in more striking color and intriguing detail.

Much of such scholarly research has occurred only in recent years. Such materials were simply not available in Joseph Smith's time, even had he been able to use them. Instead, Joseph, by his translating, was removing major stumbling blocks strewn in the path of those who would believe.

Clearly Jesus Christ, whom Joseph saw more than once, was a stumbling block to Jewish people at the time of his mortal ministry (see Jacob 4:14). The sequence in human history was set forth clearly by the prophet Nephi.

> And behold it shall come to pass that after the Messiah hath risen from the dead, and hath manifested himself unto his people, unto as many as will believe on his name, behold, Jerusalem shall be destroyed again; for wo unto them that fight against God and the people of his church.
>
> Wherefore, the Jews shall be scattered among all nations; yea, and also Babylon shall be destroyed; wherefore, the Jews shall be scattered by other nations.
>
> And after they have been scattered, and the Lord God hath scourged them by other nations for the space of many generations, yea, even down from generation to generation until they shall be persuaded to believe in Christ, the Son of God, and the atonement, which is infinite for all mankind—and when that day shall come that they shall believe in Christ, and worship the Father in his name, with pure hearts and clean hands, and look not forward any more for another Messiah, then, at that time, the day will come that it must needs be expedient that they should believe these things. (2 Nephi 25:14–16.)

"These things" refers, of course, to the word of God that was to come forth in the "other books" of scripture, especially the Book of Mormon. Obviously, this pattern of unnecessary "stumbling" is a matter of great historical significance.

Paul observed the difficulties he had in preaching Christ crucified: "But we preach Christ crucified, unto the Jews a stumbling-block, and unto the Greeks foolishness" (1 Corinthians 1:23).

Paul also noted in that connection a former prophecy that

Jesus would be a stumbling block: "Wherefore? Because they sought it not by faith, but as it were by the works of the law. For they stumbled at that stumblingstone; as it is written, Behold, I lay in Sion a stumblingstone and rock of offence: and whosoever believeth on him shall not be ashamed." (Romans 9:32–33.)

Perhaps, as Paul said, "because they sought it not by faith," Jesus was an obstacle over which many then could not climb. It is little different in our secular age.

In any event, centuries before the birth of Jesus as the Mortal Messiah he spoke to Nephi by an angel and said of the Gentiles that in the last days he would "manifest himself unto them *in word* . . . unto the taking away of their stumbling blocks" (1 Nephi 14:1; italics added). The manifestation "in word" obviously includes the "other books" of scripture, particularly the Book of Mormon. As Moses recorded, the truth is only "had again . . . among as many as shall believe" (Moses 1:41). For them, these other scriptures end the need for "an exceedingly great number [to] stumble (1 Nephi 13:29).

The Lord, who knows human nature perfectly, was well aware that there would be many religious people who would be heavily invested in the status quo; it would be difficult for them to regard his latter-day word without stumbling (see 2 Nephi 26:20).

Peter also spoke of those who "stumble *at the word*" referring, of course, to the word of God (1 Peter 2:8; italics added). Stumbling can occur because of one's not having the many "plain and precious things." Alas for some, however, the stumbling can occur at the very notion of having "other books" of scripture: "A Bible, we have got a Bible, and we need no more Bible." Says the Lord to such provincial mortals, "Know ye not that there are more nations than one? . . . know ye not that the testimony of two nations is a witness unto you?" (2 Nephi 29:6, 8.)

Those who criticize the "other books" of scripture must bear in mind that at least one cause of their stumbling was foreseen also and was worried over by contributing prophets: "Thou hast also made our words powerful and great, even that we cannot write them; wherefore, when we write we behold our weakness, and stumble because of the placing of our words; and I fear lest the Gentiles shall mock at our words" (Ether 12:25).

Some "despise" plainness and prefer complexity (see Jacob

4:14). Whatever the reason, those who treat the revelations of
God lightly will not be able to stand when "the storms descend,
and the winds blow, and the rains descend, and beat upon their
house" (see D&C 90:5).

In a stormy season, we should thus approach the Book of
Mormon and the "other books" as never before, reverently,
prayerfully, and by studying them out in our minds. Such stretching and pondering involve much more than passively noting.
Seeing relationships between various verses of scripture requires
pondering, integrating, and appreciating. Just as Joseph did in
Liberty Jail regarding many matters, when we break outside the
tiny conceptual frameworks within which we have usually read
the book, this will prepare us to be introduced by the Spirit to
precious things which, to borrow the words of Moses, we "never
had supposed" (Moses 1:10).

The fundamental reason why the Book of Mormon was written is the same motivation which caused John to write: "But these
are written, that ye might believe that Jesus is the Christ, the Son
of God; and that believing ye might have life through his name"
(John 20:31).

In the case of the Book of Mormon, what came forth was for
establishing the truth of John's words, among others, for the
"convincing" and persuading of the people that Jesus Christ
lived and yet lives, as these samples testify (italics are added in
each case):

> . . . I beheld other books, which came forth by the power of the
> Lamb, from the Gentiles unto them, unto the *convincing* of the
> Gentiles and the remnant of the seed of my brethren, and also the
> Jews . . . that the records of the prophets and of the twelve apostles
> of the Lamb are true (1 Nephi 13:39).

> But a seer will I raise up out of the fruit of thy loins; and unto
> him will I give power to bring forth my word unto the seed of thy
> loins—and not to the bringing forth my word only, saith the Lord,
> but to the *convincing* them of my word, which shall have already
> gone forth among them (2 Nephi 3:11).

> . . . And also to the *convincing* of the Jew and Gentile that Jesus
> is the Christ, the Eternal God, manifesting himself unto all nations
> (Title Page of the Book of Mormon).

Wherefore, he shall bring forth his words unto them, which words shall judge them at the last day, for they shall be given them for the purpose of *convincing* them of the true Messiah, who was rejected by them; and unto the *convincing* of them that they need not look forward any more for a Messiah to come (2 Nephi 25:18).

And as I spake concerning the *convincing* of the Jews, that Jesus is the very Christ, it must needs be that the Gentiles be *convinced* also that Jesus is the Christ, the Eternal God (2 Nephi 26:12).

And behold, they shall go unto the unbelieving of the Jews; and for this intent shall they go—that they may be *persuaded* that Jesus is the Christ, the Son of the living God; that the Father may bring about, through his most Beloved, his great and eternal purpose, in restoring the Jews, or all the house of Israel, to the land of their inheritance, which the Lord their God hath given them, unto the fulfilling of his covenant;

And also that the seed of this people may *more fully believe* his gospel, which shall go forth unto them from the Gentiles; for this people shall be scattered, and shall become a dark, a filthy, and a loathsome people, beyond the description of that which ever hath been amongst us, yea, even that which hath been among the Lamanites, and this because of their unbelief and idolatry. (Mormon 5:14–15.)

Thus the coming forth of this book carries with it powerful proof that Jesus Christ lived and yet lives. He was and is the Only Begotten Son of the Father. He is our resurrected Lord and Savior.

We should not underestimate the need for such persuading and convincing power in a world in which so many are ambivalent. Nathaniel Hawthorne said of one such friend: "It is strange how he persists . . . in wandering to and fro. . . . He can neither believe, nor be comfortable in his unbelief." (Nathaniel Hawthorne, 20 Nov. 1856, in *English Notebooks*, ed. Randall Stewart [New York: MLA], pp. 432–33.)

When all of these restored truths are combined—Jesus is the Christ, the doctrine of the premortal life, the reality of a loving Father in Heaven's plan of salvation, the reality of the resurrection—this gives those who believe them a precious perspective and purpose, "proving to the world that the holy scriptures are true, and that God does inspire men and call them to his holy

work in this age and generation, as well as in generations of old"
(D&C 20:11).

Fundamental to a man's understanding about his identity
and purpose upon this planet is to know that God has a plan of
salvation also called a plan of happiness, a plan of mercy, etc.[1]
(Alma 24:14; 42:8; 42:15). Yet there are no references to "a plan"
of salvation as such in the Old or the New Testament, though
there are implied and oblique references. Consider the conveying
simplicity of the word *plan*.

There are multiple references to the plan of salvation in the
latter-day "other books" of modern scripture, as these extracted
lines demonstrate:

> For as death hath passed upon all men, to fulfil the merciful
> plan of the great Creator, there must needs be a power of resurrec-
> tion (2 Nephi 9:6).

> Now, if it had not been for the plan of redemption, which was
> laid from the foundation of the world (Alma 12:25).

> But God did call on men, in the name of his Son, (this being the
> plan of redemption which was laid) (Alma 12:33).

> And Aaron did expound . . . the plan of redemption, which
> was prepared from the foundation of the world (Alma 22:13).

> For according to the great plan of the Eternal God there must
> be an atonement made (Alma 34:9).

> For behold, if Adam had put forth his hand immediately, and
> partaken of the tree of life, . . . the great plan of salvation would
> have been frustrated (Alma 42:5).

> . . . for that would destroy the great plan of happiness (Alma
> 42:8).

> And now, the plan of mercy could not be brought about except
> an atonement should be made (Alma 42:15).

> And now, behold, I say unto you: This is the plan of salvation
> unto all men (Moses 6:62).

> And the Gods saw that they would be obeyed, and that their
> plan was good (Abraham 4:21).

These constitute a stunning supply of plain truths about
God's *plan* and cardinal concepts which truly "grow together"
concerning man's purposes on this planet. They "establish" the

words of Isaiah: "For thus saith the Lord that created the
heavens; God himself that formed the earth and made it; he hath
established it, he created it not in vain, he formed it to be inhab-
ited" (Isaiah 45:18).

We do, of course, receive vital biblical information concerning the importance of the atoning Christ and eternal life.

> Neither is there salvation in any other: for there is none other
> name under heaven given among men, whereby we must be saved
> (Acts 4:12).

> For as in Adam all die, even so in Christ shall all be made alive
> (1 Corinthians 15:22).

> In hope of eternal life, which God, that cannot lie, promised
> before the world began (Titus 1:2).

> And being made perfect, he became the author of eternal
> salvation unto all them that obey him (Hebrews 5:9).

> Who verily was foreordained before the foundation of the
> world, but was manifest in these last times for you (1 Peter 1:20).

> For for this cause was the gospel preached also to them that are
> dead, that they might be judged according to men in the flesh, but
> live according to God in the spirit (1 Peter 4:6).

Important and helpful as these scriptures are, however, they
do not give us a fulness concerning God's plan of salvation, such
as was revealed to the Prophet Joseph—including his revelations
in the jail—concerning plans laid in the Grand Council of the
Eternal God before this world was.

One has only to ponder what a striking difference the gospel
fulness would make for so many mortals who now view themselves and this life so existentially and provincially. How glorious
if these individuals were willing to understand that (1) God has a
plan of salvation of which this second estate—or mortality—is a
key part; (2) "men are that they might have joy"; (3) we are truly
accountable for our thoughts, words, and deeds while here; (4)
the resurrection is a reality; and (5) a loving Father is seeing us
through this mortal schooling as our Schoolmaster.

Such knowledge and understanding would not put an end to
human imperfection but it would put an end to ultimate uncer-
tainty on the pathway to salvation, making possible tremendous

shifts in attitudes and behavior for immense numbers of people on this planet.

Lacking these "plain and precious" truths, however, life seems to be a puzzle for many, lacking in meaning and comprehensibility.

The "light of Christ," which to some degree lights all mortals, often causes an intrinsic and positive response when gospel doctrine is taught (see D&C 84:46; John 1:9).

Those who wish to become true disciples and true believers can ensure that they do not become "wearied and faint in [their] minds" (Hebrews 12:3), if they will feast upon Jesus' doctrines in their fulness and thus comprehend how God's redemptive plan exists and persists. Oh, the emancipation there is in revelation!

All of these things, of course, are a witness to divine design but also to the loving intent which motivated laboring and bequeathing ancestors and prophets. These prophet-predecessors truly cared about communicating with us in our time.

> Now in this thing we do rejoice; and we labor diligently to engraven these words upon plates, hoping that our beloved brethren and our children will receive them with thankful hearts, and look upon them that they may learn with joy and not with sorrow, neither with contempt, concerning their first parents (Jacob 4:3).
>
> For behold, this [the Book of Mormon] is written for the intent that ye may believe that [the Bible]; and if ye believe that ye will believe this also; and if ye believe this ye will know concerning your fathers, and also the marvelous works which were wrought by the power of God among them (Mormon 7:9).

Actual revelation concerning us and our time permitted the comments of these ancient prophets to be made with relevant awareness of our needs and challenging circumstances. In the words of Moroni: "Behold, I speak unto you as if ye were present, and yet ye are not. But behold, Jesus Christ hath shown you unto me, and I know your doing." (Mormon 8:35.)

Again, the caution must be given that the most important witness of the authenticity of the Book of Mormon is the witness of the Spirit. Lehi's report of his ancestor Joseph's prophecies and the inspired foresight of Book of Mormon prophets, to the effect that these various books of scripture would "grow together" (2

Nephi 3:12), signified a many-sided development. This growing together would no doubt embrace the efforts of the Latter-day Saint scholars in uncovering and integrating external evidences— after all, "to be learned is good if they hearken unto the counsels of God" (2 Nephi 9:29). But much more significant would be the vast amount of internal evidence and witness that would increasingly surrender its treasures to the eager mind and heart, especially as these faculties would become trained in spiritual perceptions and thus would tap into the teaching resources of the Spirit. Such a combination would provide an enlarged foundation upon which all believers could place even greater reliance, with greater utilization of the truths in these books: "That every man might speak in the name of God the Lord, even the Savior of the world" (D&C 1:20). False doctrines would also be confounded. Contentions would be put down. Peace would finally be established "among the fruit of [Joseph's] loins" (1 Nephi 3:12), as the various descendants of Israel acquired a knowledge of their fathers and of the Lord's covenants.

Another promise was given in that same chapter. Though he translated the words, Joseph may not at that time have realized their full implications. The promise was and is that those who would try to destroy the work of the latter-day seer "shall be confounded" (2 Nephi 3:14). One of the ways in which this promise continues to be kept, of course, is the absence of successful, substantive challenge to the massive, complex translations and revelations which came through Joseph Smith.

As one begins to appreciate further the Book of Mormon, both as a historical record and as a witnessing, religious volume, another parallel out of human history comes to mind. In the book, earnest prophets who witnessed social deterioration, including terrible slaughters, were moved upon to make a record of those things.

> But behold, the land was filled with robbers and with Lamanites; and notwithstanding the great destruction which hung over my people, they did not repent of their evil doings; therefore there was blood and carnage spread throughout all the face of the land, both on the part of the Nephites and also on the part of the Lamanites; and it was one complete revolution throughout all the face of the land (Mormon 2:8).

> And it came to pass that my sorrow did return unto me again, and I saw that the day of grace was passed with them, both temporally and spiritually; for I saw thousands of them hewn down in open rebellion against their God, and heaped up as dung upon the face of the land. And thus three hundred and forty and four years had passed away. (Mormon 2:15.)

For Mormon, seeing thousands of bodies "heaped up as dung upon the face of the land" must have produced profound emotions within him, not unlike those a British journalist experienced when he went to the Bergen-Belsen concentration camp at the end of World War II, the opening lines of whose dispatch were, "It is my duty to describe something beyond the imagination of mankind" (*Time Magazine*, April 29, 1985, p. 133—International Edition).

Again, the words of Mormon: "And it is impossible for the tongue to describe, or for man to write a perfect description of the horrible scene of the blood and carnage which was among the people, both of the Nephites and of the Lamanites; and every heart was hardened, so that they delighted in the shedding of blood continually" (Mormon 4:11).

The anticipating, foreknowing, integrating pattern of God's bringing things forward—at the moment in time when they are most needed—is surely to be seen regarding the convergence and relevance of the Bible and these "other books." Hence our faith in the Lord must include not only faith that he exists but also faith in his timing as his purposes unfold.

Perhaps our previous failure to notice some of these things can be partly attributed to the way in which the Book of Mormon deliberately understates certain things. When these are discovered, it will be by the meek who have eyes to see. It should not surprise us, therefore, as the climate of criticism intensifies concerning the Church, the Prophet Joseph Smith, the Book of Mormon, temples, and so on, that the Lord will focus our attention and deepen our appreciation in order to preserve a climate in which his work will go forward even more rapidly among those who are honest in heart.

Things "shall grow together." Believers will be astounded. Those who seek to tear down the Lord's work will be frustrated. (See 2 Nephi 3:14.)

It all commenced, however, as the "choice seer" was in the presence of Heavenly Beings who "called" him and others "to a dispensation of [the] gospel in the beginning of the fullness of times," just as Joseph declared from Liberty Jail (*Writings*, p. 399).

Given all that was accomplished earlier, it is no wonder that the Lord profitably used even the period of Joseph's confinement. In our day too the Lord will likewise use the attacks on his latter-day seer to push Joseph's work and name even further out to the ends of the earth.

Notes

1. Joseph Smith, Sr., had a dream in 1811, in which he found himself traveling in a barren field covered with dead fallen timber. "Not a vestige of life, either animal or vegetable, could be seen; besides, to render the scene still more dreary, the most death-like silence prevailed, no sound of anything animate could be heard in all the field." What did this silent, lifeless desert represent? The attendant spirit told him that "this field is the world which now lieth inanimate and dumb, in regard to the true religion or plan of salvation." (Bushman, pp. 38–39.)

CHAPTER 4

"Called and Prepared from the Foundation of the World" Alma 13:3

One unique and powerful doctrine earlier restored through Joseph the Seer was amplified by revelations received in the prison-temple. It provides a special and obvious example of how lost truths can actually become a deprivation and a diversion that constitute a stumbling block (1 Nephi 13:40; 14:1). This doctrine is the truth about the premortal existence of men and women—existence as individual personalities and entities. The general absence of this deep doctrine and this precious perspective has had a profound and inevitable effect upon the way in which many mortals view this life. Indeed, the loss of this doctrine in its plainness and fulness has been a subtle stumbling block to many without their even sensing it.

Clearly the doctrine of premortal existence of individuals is a key to understanding the Lord's plan of salvation. Much of the human despair about the meaning of life and the perplexities of the mortal condition stems from being unaware or unbelieving of the reality of this precious doctrine.

For many years now—in literature, film, and music—we have witnessed increasing expressions of a profound sense of existential despair, a hopelessness seemingly beyond hope. Granted, the human scene also includes many individuals who go happily about life's labors untouched by these feelings, drawing upon "the light of Christ" which, to a degree, lights every individual (see D&C 84:46; Moroni 7:16; John 1:9). Thus some individuals

have intrinsic intimations which sustain them. Even so, the holo-
causts and wars have taken their terrible toll of hope among
twentieth-century man. Said one eminent scientist: "The most
poignant problem of modern life is probably man's feeling that
life has lost its significance . . . [A] view . . . no longer limited to
the philosophical or literary *avant garde*. It is spreading to all
social and economic groups and affects all manifestations of life."
(Rene Dubos, *So Human an Animal* [New York: Scribners, 1968],
pp. 14–15.)

One need not question, either, the reluctance or sincerity
with which some despairing individuals have come to such wrong
conclusions. In fact, one feels compassion.

One recent television drama, its closing scene in a cemetery,
conveyed well this confusion and purposelessness as a character
lamented poignantly: "Are all men's lives . . . broken, tumultu-
ous, agonized and unromantic, punctuated by screams, imbecili-
ties, agonies and death? Who knows? . . . I don't know. . . . Why
can't people have what they want? The things were all there to
content everybody, yet everybody got the wrong thing. I don't
know. It's beyond me. It's all darkness." (PBS production of *The
Good Soldier*, dramatization of the novel by Ford Madox Ford.)

But such poignancy is not a guarantee of accuracy.

Alas, however, in human affairs such erroneous and unchal-
lenged assertions sometimes assume an undeserved aura of
reality, as with absorbed children in a treehouse pretending they
are brave and alone. While the restored gospel's reassuring
response to this hopelessness may not create conviction in all disbelievers, it has helped and will help many as well as bolstering
believers against the silent erosion of their convictions.

Let us, therefore, place several such lamentations beside the
revelations of God, so many of which came through the "choice
seer," Joseph Smith. Let us place the expressions of despair
beside the divine annunciations of hope; the fears of extinction
alongside the reassurances of the resurrection; the expressions of
provincialism beside the universalism of the gospel of Jesus
Christ. Then we shall see how myopic some mortals are. No
wonder some lament that man spends his entire life trying to
prove to himself that his existence is not absurd!

The lamentations: Man lives in "an unsponsored universe," a universe "without a master," which "cares nothing for [man's] hopes and fears," an "empire of chance" in which man falls victim to "the trampling march of unconscious power." (Bertrand Russell, "A Free Man's Worship," in *Mysticism and Logic and Other Essays* [London: George Allen and Unwin, Ltd., 1950], p. 57.)

The revelations:

God himself that formed the earth . . . created it not in vain, he formed it to be inhabited (Isaiah 45:18).

For he is our God; and we are the people of his pasture, and the sheep of his hand (Psalm 95:7).

Behold, this is my work and my glory—to bring to pass the immortality and eternal life of man (Moses 1:39).

Men are, that they might have joy (2 Nephi 2:25).

But the very hairs of your head are all numbered (Matthew 10:29–30).

But only an account of this earth, and the inhabitants thereof, give I unto you. For behold, there are many worlds that have passed away by the word of my power. And there are many that now stand, and innumerable are they unto man; but all things are numbered unto me, for they are mine and I know them. (Moses 1:35.)

The fears: Mankind is "destined to extinction. . . . There is nothing we can do." "We have no personal life beyond the grave. There is no God. Fate knows no wrath nor ruth [compassion]." (James Thompson, *The City of Dreadful Night and Other Poems* [London: Bertram Dobell, 1899], pp. 29–30, 35–36.)

The reassurances:

And the graves were opened; and many bodies of the saints which slept arose,

And came out of the graves after his resurrection, and went into the holy city, and appeared unto many. (Matthew 27:52–53; see also 3 Nephi 23:9–11.)

O death, where is thy sting? O grave, where is thy victory? (1 Corinthians 15:55.)

O how great the plan of our God! (2 Nephi 9:13.)

> For we saw him, even on the right hand of God; and we heard
> the voice bearing record that he is the Only Begotten of the Father—
>   That by him, and through him, and of him, the worlds are and
> were created, and the inhabitants thereof are begotten sons and
> daughters unto God. (D&C 76:23–24.)

The reality of premortality is thus a curative for the wonder-
ings, puzzlings, and yearnings expressed in music, poetry, and
literature, such as the following:

> Everything in our life happens as though we entered upon it
> with a load of obligations contracted in a previous existence. . . .
> obligations whose sanction is not of this present life, [which] seem
> to belong to a different world, founded on kindness, scruples, sacri-
> fice, a world entirely different from this one, a world whence we
> emerge to be born on this earth, before returning thither." (Marcel
> Proust, *La Prisonniere*, as quoted in *Homo Viator*, by Gabriel
> Marcel [New York: Harper and Row, 1963], p. 8.)

Some who despair, as Peter said, "willingly are ignorant" (2
Peter 3:5). Others, as Nephi pointed out, "will not search . . . nor
understand great knowledge" (2 Nephi 32:7). For some, a pessi-
mistic philosophy is actually "pleasing unto the carnal mind"
(Alma 30:53). Happily, still others, no doubt fired by that in
which they do not believe—the light of Christ which lights every
soul—live decent lives anyway.

Alas, behavioral permissiveness flourishes amid a sense of
hopelessness. If human appetites are mistakenly viewed as the
only authentic reality, and "now" as the only moment that
matters, why should one checkrein any impulse or defer any
gratification? Hence individual accountability and belief in individual immortality are intertwined.

There are biblical references to the doctrine of premortal existence. But these are not so numerous as to preclude some Christians from ignoring them or still others from attempting to explain
them away. Just how many prophetic utterances concerning
these doctrines were mislaid, "held back" or "taken away" from
the early records from which we later received the precious Holy
Bible, we know not.

When biblical scriptures bear directly upon this vitally important doctrine, sometimes it is by citing, here and there, a premor-

tal existence wherein there were differences as between the forces of evil and those of righteousness. Satan led the forces of evil.

And he said unto them, I beheld Satan as lightning fall from heaven (Luke 1:18).

And there was war in heaven: Michael and his angels fought against the dragon; and the dragon fought and his angels (Revelation 12:7; see JST Revelation 12:6–8).

And the angels which kept not their first estate, but left their own habitation, he hath reserved in everlasting chains under darkness unto the judgment of the great day (Jude 1:6).

The "other books" of scripture (1 Nephi 13:39–40), however, give *plain* as well as *precious* confirmation and elaboration. They offer these more clear-cut references:

Wherefore, because that Satan rebelled against me, and sought to destroy the agency of man, which I, the Lord God, had given him, and also, that I should give unto him mine own power; by the power of mine Only Begotten, I caused that he should be cast down (Moses 4:3).

And it came to pass that Adam, being tempted of the devil—for, behold, the devil was before Adam, for he rebelled against me, saying, Give me thine honor, which is my power; and also a third part of the hosts of heaven turned he away from me because of their agency (D&C 29:36).

And this we saw also, and bear record, that an angel of God who was in authority in the presence of God, who rebelled against the Only Begotten Son whom the Father loved and who was in the bosom of the Father, was thrust down from the presence of God and the Son (D&C 76:25).

And I, Lehi, according to the things which I have read, must needs suppose that an angel of God, according to that which is written, had fallen from heaven; wherefore, he became a devil, having sought that which was evil before God.

And because he had fallen from heaven, and had become miserable forever, he sought also the misery of all mankind. Wherefore, he said unto Eve, yea, even that old serpent, who is the devil, who is the father of all lies, wherefore he said: Partake of the forbidden fruit, and ye shall not die, but ye shall be as God, knowing good and evil. (2 Nephi 2:17–18.)

One biblical reference to the premortal existence of man appears in this instructive episode: "And his disciples asked him, saying, Master, who did sin, this man, or his parents, that he was born blind?" (John 9:2.)

Significantly, Jesus did not rebuke the disciples for advancing "either/or" premises, but said, "Neither." "Jesus answered, Neither hath this man sinned, nor his parents: but that the works of God should be made manifest in him" (John 9:3).

Since teachings about premortal existence were "abroad in the land" in Jesus' day,[1] he could have very easily corrected the assumptions the questioning disciples had. Rather, he indicated that the blindness was neither the result of the man's sinning before he was born nor of his parents' sinning; rather, the works of God were made manifest in the blind man, and not simply to provide an object lesson in healing.

All the biblical scriptures are seen with fresher, clearer vision when placed in the light of the "other books" of scripture wherein these truths about man's *continuum of existence* are stated—but more clearly and plainly:

> Now the Lord had shown unto me, Abraham, the intelligences that were organized before the world was; and among all these there were many of the noble and great ones;
> And God saw these souls that they were good, and he stood in the midst of them, and he said: These I will make my rulers; for he stood among those that were spirits, and he saw that they were good; and he said unto me: Abraham, thou art one of them; thou wast chosen before thou wast born. (Abraham 3:22–23.) (See Psalm 82:1—New English Bible, The Jerusalem Bible, and the Anchor Bible Series.)

> But behold, the resurrection of Christ redeemeth mankind, yea, even all mankind, and bringeth them back into the presence of the Lord (Helaman 14:17).

> And that it might be filled with the measure of man, according to his creation before the world was made (D&C 49:17).

> Man was also in the beginning with God. Intelligence, or the light of truth, was not created or made, neither indeed can be. (D&C 93:29.)

> The Prophet Joseph Smith, and my father, Hyrum Smith, Brigham Young, John Taylor, Wilford Woodruff, and other choice

spirits who were reserved to come forth in the fulness of times to take part in laying the foundations of the great latter-day work, . . .

I observed that they were also among the noble and great ones who were chosen in the beginning to be rulers in the Church of God.

Even before they were born, they, with many others, received their first lessons in the world of spirits and were prepared to come forth in the due time of the Lord to labor in his vineyard for the salvation of the souls of men. (D&C 138:53, 55–56.)

Many other references in the "other books" of scripture "grow together," and thus speak more plainly and powerfully of God's plan of salvation (see previous chapter) and of man's purposeful coming here to be proved and to be trained.

Our purposeful coming here reflects a premortal existence (a first estate) in which man had reached a point when, in the wisdom of God, this second estate became necessary to prepare man for a third and final resurrected estate wherein he might be "added upon" (see Abraham 3:25–26). The scriptures therefore contain numerous pointed references to the tutoring and refining process of life:

Nevertheless the Lord seeth fit to chasten his people; yea, he trieth their patience and their faith (Mosiah 23:21).

And we will prove them herewith, to see if they will do all things whatsoever the Lord their God shall command them (Abraham 3:25). (For other references on "proving" see Exodus 16:4; Deuteronomy 8:2, 16; 13:3.)

Obviously, for the plan of salvation to unfold in an orderly manner and to accomplish the ordained purposes of God, he must, as Paul indicated, "determine . . . the bounds of their habitation" beforehand (Acts 17:26).

Joseph Smith taught: "Every man who has a calling to minister to the inhabitants of the world was ordained to that very purpose in the Grand Council of heaven before this world was. I suppose I was ordained to this very office in that Grand Council." (*Teachings*, p. 365.) We do not read of Joseph's so speaking until after Liberty Jail, for it was in that prison-temple that revelation came concerning the Council of the Eternal God (D&C 121:32). However, since in 1838 Joseph wrote, of his 1820 vision, "many other things did [the Savior] say unto me, which I cannot write at this time," we cannot be sure he first heard of this council in 1839 (see JS–H 1:20).

The comments in Jeremiah 1:5 clearly and unequivocally speak of Jeremiah's foreordination as "a prophet unto the nations." The biblical example of foreordination is a direct evidence of the truthfulness of what we read in the book of Abraham.

> Now the Lord had shown unto me, Abraham, the intelligences that were organized before the world was; and among all these there were many of the noble and great ones;
>
> And God saw these souls that they were good, and he stood in the midst of them, and he said: These I will make my rulers; for he stood among those that were spirits, and he saw that they were good; and he said unto me: Abraham, thou art one of them; thou wast chosen before thou wast born. (Abraham 3:22–23.)

With such foreknowledge as to both souls and roles, God would "set the bounds of the people" (Deuteronomy 32:8; see also Genesis 10:32) and make determinations as to chronology—what Paul called "the times before appointed" (Acts 17:26).

Paul clearly preached the doctrine of foreordination: "For whom he did foreknow, he also did predestinate[2] to be conformed to the image of his Son, that he might be the firstborn among many brethren" (Romans 8:29).

How could God foreknow a people unless they existed before their birth here? "God hath not cast away his people which he foreknew. Wot ye not what the scripture saith of Elias? how he maketh intercession to God against Israel. . . ." (Romans 11:2.)

Paul similarly declared: "According as he hath chosen us in him before the foundation of the world, that we should be holy and without blame before him in love. Having predestinated[3] us unto the adoption of children by Jesus Christ to himself, according to the good pleasure of his will." (Ephesians 1:4–5.)

This doctrine, therefore, did not apply solely to Jesus or Jeremiah:

> But we are bound to give thanks alway to God for you, brethren beloved of the Lord, because God hath from the beginning chosen you to salvation through sanctification of the Spirit and belief of the truth (2 Thessalonians 2:13).

> Who hath saved us, and called us with an holy calling, not according to our works, but according to his own purpose and grace, which was given us in Christ Jesus before the world began . . . (2 Timothy 1:9).

Peter likewise preached the doctrines of foreknowledge and foreordination: "Elect according to the foreknowledge of God the Father, through sanctification of the Spirit, unto obedience and sprinkling of the blood of Jesus Christ: Grace unto you, and peace, be multiplied." (1 Peter 1:2.)

Thus we see that God's foreknowledge and the doctrine of foreordination go together. (See Blake Ostler, "Clothed Upon: A Unique Aspect of Christian Antiquity," *BYU Studies,* vol. 22, no. 1 [Winter 1982], pp. 31–33.) The one makes the other possible, as a loving Father in Heaven executes his plan of salvation for his children, desiring, as his glory, our salvation and our happiness.

As just illustrated, the Holy Bible contains much more pertaining to the precious, plain doctrine of the premortal existence than many realize. But appropriately the fulness has been restored in the fulness of times.

This doctrine is a major example of a key doctrine which for various reasons and causes did not make its way *fully* into the Holy Bible. The devoted and talented King James scholars loyally and effectively translated that work from the materials at hand, but they could not translate that which had been previously "held back." What we have as surviving verses on this subject, though the Bible itself has been of immeasurable value to Christendom through the centuries, does not represent the fulness.

Some scholars and preachers attempt to confine the doctrine of premortal existence to Jesus only—with Lucifer in one scene. This results in an enormous distortion of reality which carries with it tremendous consequences for mankind. In many ways, it is the equivalent of saying, "Yes, Jesus was resurrected, but the resurrection only applies to him and not to all the rest of us." To attempt to strip away from all the rest of us the reality of our premortal existence is to rob us of our identity, to lessen our full accountability, and to dim our perspectives concerning ourselves and the purposes of life.

Although our Bible does not spell out a premortal life, it contains some bracing references to God's being the Father of our spirits.

> And they fell upon their faces, and said, O God, the God of the spirits of all flesh, shall one man sin, and wilt thou be wroth with all the congregation? (Numbers 16:22.)

> Then shall the dust return to the earth as it was: and the spirit shall return unto God who gave it (Ecclesiastes 12:7).

> The burden of the word of the Lord for Israel, saith the Lord, which stretcheth forth the heavens, and layeth the foundation of the earth, and formeth the spirit of man within him (Zechariah 12:1).

> Furthermore we have had fathers of our flesh which corrected us, and we gave them reverence: shall we not much rather be in subjection unto the Father of spirits, and live? (Hebrews 12:9.)

Once again, the "other books" give us both verification and clarification:

> Man was also in the beginning with God. Intelligence, or the light of truth, was not created or made, neither indeed can be. (D&C 93:29.)

> But behold, the resurrection of Christ redeemeth mankind, yea, even all mankind, and bringeth them back into the presence of the Lord (Helaman 14:17).

> And that it might be filled with the measure of man, according to his creation before the world was made (D&C 49:17).

In the aggregate these further attestations to the premortal existence of man point directly and consistently to the shared reality of our having lived as individual entities before coming to this life. Jesus, the Father's designated leader there, is our Savior here.

Long before Joseph Smith's time, what had failed to be included in the Bible was lost, and ancient documents bearing upon such matters had not yet emerged. Hugh Nibley has observed: "Few people realize that in Joseph Smith's day *no* really ancient manuscripts were known. Egyptian and Babylonian could not be read; the Greek and Latin classics were the oldest literature available. . . . The oldest text of the Hebrew Bible was the Ben Asher Codex from the ninth century A.D. Today we have whole libraries of documents more than four thousand years old

—not just their contents, but the actual writings themselves going back to the very beginnings of civilization." (*Timely and Timeless,* pp. 103–4.)[4]

Interestingly enough some recently available historical evidence indicates that, while the doctrine of premortal existence did not survive in full abundance to take its place in the Holy Bible, it was taught by some during and after the apostolic era in the meridian of time. In fact, it was not until A.D. 553, and perhaps a few years prior, that (by the action of the Second Council of Constantinople) teachers of this doctrine were declared "anathema" (see Adolf Harnack, *History of Dogma,* vol. IV [New York: Dover Publishers, 1961], pp. 245, 347–49; also Philip Hughes, *The Church in Crisis: A History of the General Councils, 325–1870* [Garden City, NY: Doubleday, 1964], pp. 117–18).

The Nag Hammadi library gives us some information in the Apocryphon[5] of James, Codex I (about A.D. 150) from a Gnostic document. Jesus is there quoted as saying to Peter and James, while speaking of the extent of the two disciples' sufferings, "If you consider how long the world existed [before] you fell [into it] and how long it will exist after you, you will find that your life is a single day and your sufferings a single hour."

Many of Origen's writings are certainly lost to us because his teachings were condemned. Blake Ostler has written, "When Origen stated, 'We believe that other worlds existed before the present world came into being,' he was not expressing a personal opinion, instead he seemed to be stating an article of faith belonging to the Christian church of his day." (From unpublished paper, April 10, 1981, and letter to author, October 4, 1985, citing Alexander Roberts and James Donaldson, *Ante-Nicene Fathers* [Grand Rapids: Christian Lit. Co., 1893], 5:341.)

It is striking that, similar to what we find in the book of Abraham, Origen described the variety of man's mortal circumstances as having some relationship to their lives before coming here.[6] Unsurprisingly, it resembles what Alma sets forth:

> And this is the manner after which they were ordained—being called and prepared from the foundation of the world according to the foreknowledge of God, on account of their exceeding faith and

good works; in the first place being left to choose good or evil; therefore they having chosen good, and exercising exceedingly great faith, are called with a holy calling, yea, with that holy calling which was prepared with, and according to, a preparatory redemption for such.

Or in fine, in the first place they were on the same standing with their brethren; thus this holy calling being prepared from the foundation of the world for such as would not harden their hearts, being in and through the atonement of the Only Begotten Son, who was prepared. (Alma 13:3, 5.)

Further light comes from the book of Abraham:

Howbeit that he made the greater star; as, also, if there be two spirits, and one shall be more intelligent than the other, yet these two spirits, notwithstanding one is more intelligent than the other, have no beginning; they existed before, they shall have no end, they shall exist after, for they are gnolaum, or eternal.

And the Lord said unto me: These two facts do exist, that there are two spirits, one being more intelligent than the other; there shall be another more intelligent than they; I am the Lord thy God, I am more intelligent than they all. (Abraham 3:18–19.)

The Talmud and the Midrash clearly teach the doctrine of the premortal existence of souls. In another Jewish book, "God is represented as taking counsel with the souls of the righteous before he created the earth" (James Hastings, *Encyclopaedia of Religion and Ethics*, 1:x. [New York: Charles Scribner's Sons, 1924]).

Justin Martyr (A.D. 100–167) also taught this doctrine, including the concept that if men "by their good works prove themselves worthy of His plan they are considered worthy . . . to return to His presence and reign with Him" (Justin Martyr, *Apologia I pro Christianis*, 10 Greek text, in J. P. Migne, *Patrologiae Graecae* 161 vols. [Paris: n.p., 1857–68], 6:340F).

Critics of this doctrine, of course, are quick to say that Justin Martyr was a Platonist before his conversion and simply brought that doctrine with him. Others are quick to pass off the episode in which Jesus and his disciples encountered the blind man as merely being evidence that the disciples were otherwise aware of the doctrine of the premortal existence. Such an approach leaves Jesus' stunning reply, full of implications, without a response.

Clement, Bishop of Rome, who was acquainted with the original Apostles, in a somewhat helpful passage urged his members, "Let us consider, therefore, brethren, whereof we are made, who and what kind of men we came into the world . . . [God] that made us, and formed us, brought us into His own world having presented us with His benefits, even before we were born" (*I Clement*, xxxviii, 3–4, p. 1:285, following the translation of Robert M. Grant and Holt Grahm, *The Apostolic Fathers* 2:67; see also *Lost Books of the Bible* [New York: Bell Publishing, 1979], p. 130).

Blake Ostler in the previously cited *BYU Studies* article (vol. 22, pp. 31–33) discusses how various early writings provide us with confirmation that this doctrine was taught anciently.

Origen wrote about present blessings being related to previous obedience, recognizing that if individuals were elected "not on the grounds of justice and according to their deserts, but undeservedly," then God would be a respecter of persons (*De Principiis* I, vii.4; cf. III, v.4–5). Note the parallels in modern scripture:

> There is a law, irrevocably decreed in heaven before the foundations of this world, upon which all blessings are predicated—
> And when we obtain any blessing from God, it is by obedience to that law upon which it is predicated. (D&C 130:20–21.)

> For all who will have a blessing at my hands shall abide the law which was appointed for that blessing, and the conditions thereof, as were instituted from before the foundation of the world (D&C 132:5).

Unfortunately the time came, as Paul had prophesied, when early Church members could not endure this or other sound doctrine, and the truth gave place to fables (see 2 Timothy 4:3).

Happily, for what we know of this precious doctrine we are not dependent on research—but on *revelation!*

Hugh Nibley has stressed that the doctrine of premortal existence is related to the plurality of worlds. We know that Jesus has created innumerable worlds besides this one.

> All things were made by him; and without him was not any thing made that was made (John 1:3).

[God] hath in these last days spoken unto us by his Son, whom he hath appointed heir of all things, by whom also he made the worlds (Hebrews 1:2).

The comparative clarity of latter-day revelations is, as always, impressive:

That by him, and through him, and of him, the worlds are and were created, and the inhabitants thereof are begotten sons and daughters unto God (D&C 76:24).

And worlds without number have I created; and I also created them for mine own purpose; and by the Son I created them, which is mine Only Begotten. . . .

But only an account of this earth, and the inhabitants thereof, give I unto you. For behold, there are many worlds that have passed away by the word of my power. And there are many that now stand, and innumerable are they unto man; but all things are numbered unto me, for they are mine and I know them. . . .

And as one earth shall pass away, and the heavens thereof even so shall another come; and there is no end to my works, neither to my words. (Moses 1:33, 35, 38.)

Granted, the ordering simplicity of the doctrines of premortal existence and plurality of worlds offends some. They would rather continue to engage in bewailing the human condition, or in eating, drinking, and being merry while life lasts and before man is extinguished, like victims of amnesia strangely uninterested in their pasts.

Latter-day Saints do not, of course, ask others to accept such truths against their wills. We seek tolerance for our gospel views, not involuntary agreement with them. We fully expect such doctrines to be scrutinized and even criticized by others. We reserve the same freedom to engage in scrutiny of their beliefs. All in mutual good will, however.

Neither do we ask others to believe this doctrine because it is comforting—only because it is true! In fact, premortality is not an easy doctrine. Like other central truths in the gospel of Jesus Christ, it is a hard saying (see John 6:60, 66). It brings much-needed identity but also much accountability.

It is a *plain* and *precious* doctrine, however. Those of us in the restored Church have an obligation and duty to share—with all who have eyes to see and ears to hear—that which is essential to our understanding the purposes of life, our own identity, and the very ground of our being.

Thus do the "other books" (the Book of Mormon, the Pearl of Great Price, the Doctrine and Covenants, and Joseph Smith's incomplete but inspired translation of the Bible) provide a comparative fulness of understanding concerning this and other doctrines. This is a fulness which constitutes a pivotal contribution to beleagured, provincial mankind. It came to us, via translation and revelation, through Joseph Smith, and the prison-temple played a part in its enhancement and articulation.

One of the significant developments we see in the ministry of the Prophet Joseph Smith is how, for instance, his reading of the book of Genesis for the purpose of better translation catapulted him, and therefore us, into further understanding. Though we lack details of the experience, it was out of this effort that we were to receive through revelation to the "choice seer" the remarkable book of Moses with its many special insights related to premortality and the plurality of God's creations.

Did this process of supplying additional scriptures operate as revelation did in the case of the prophet Samuel (see 1 Samuel 9:15), when "the Lord . . . told Samuel in his ear"? Or was it by Joseph's seeing replacement words on a page? We do not know in every instance whether it was visual, aural, or otherwise. But the enlargement was real, because it carried Joseph Smith not only beyond what was then available, but in the case of the doctrine of premortality beyond what was even under discussion.

Joseph's awareness of these doctrines may have ripened from recognition to appreciation of them long before he began to speak about them. The ripening which led to understanding could not have been instantaneous. True, the words earlier fell from his lips as he translated or dictated. But later on the words came from his heart, and the revealed truths became his own.

In fact, in the early days of the Restoration, these concepts arrived like dinner guests, nearly all at once. There was scarcely time to greet them. Only later was there time truly to get acquainted. Then the Prophet-host learned of the relationships of these "dinner guests" and of the antiquity of their credentials.

The arriving all at once is best illustrated by how closely

grouped they were by approximate chronology. Further, it is instructive to "line up" in this way the various scriptures which came through the Prophet Joseph concerning our premortal existence, whether by revelation or translation:

Mid-1829—2 Nephi 2:17–18 (the devil is a fallen angel)

Mid-1829—2 Nephi 9:8, 9, 16 (the devil is a fallen angel and our spirits can become subject to him)

Mid-1829—Mosiah 3:6 (evil spirits can dwell in mortals)

Mid-1829—Alma 13:2–5 (some mortals were called and prepared from the foundation of the world)

June 1830—Moses 1:33–34 (other worlds were created for a purpose and Adam as the first man of all men)

September 1830—D&C 29:28, 36, 40, 42 (about devils, angels, and how a third of the hosts of heaven fell because of the misuse of their agency and became subject to the devil and his angels)

June-October 1830—Moses 3:4–5 (about the spiritual creation of all things before they were naturally upon the earth)

June-October 1830—Moses 4:1–4 (Satan's premortal bid for power and Jesus' accepting of the Father's plan; the rebellion in heaven)

June-October 1830—Moses 5:24 (Lucifer's premortal role)

March 1831—D&C 49:17 (man was created before the world was)

February 16, 1832—D&C 76:25–28 (Satan's premortal rebellion)

May 6, 1833—D&C 93:29, 33, 38 (a most clear-cut statement of premortal existence)

1842—(the book of Abraham published, which speaks of "the intelligences that were organized before the world was" [see Abraham 3:22])

All of the above scriptures except the book of Abraham came very early in Joseph's ministry. Yet there is an apparent "gap" of six years before the Prophet began to speak or write publicly of the doctrine of premortal existence. Whether this reflected imperfect record-keeping, the Lord's timing, Joseph's degree of readiness, or the people's readiness to receive, or all such factors, we do not know. But it is clear that since the revelations came incrementally, Joseph's understanding came likewise.

Finally, just over two months before the martyrdom, there came the soaring King Follett sermon—April 7, 1844. Joseph then declared, among many things, "If men do not comprehend the character of God, they do not comprehend themselves" (*Teachings*, p. 343).

The highly knowledgeable Apostle John wrote about the final triumph of the Lord's people and how, finally, "they that are with" Christ will be those who are "called, and chosen, and faithful" (Revelation 17:14). From the Apostle Joseph, however, we receive needed and added light and knowledge about what the phrase "called and prepared from the foundation of the world" meant!

Such revelations signaled the end of a long darkness in human history, a scarcity like that in another time during which "the word of the Lord was precious . . . ; there was no open vision" (1 Samuel 3:1). This powerful doctrine of a premortal life was made plain and was esteemed as precious by Joseph who, like Jeremiah, was long before his mortal birth "ordained . . . a prophet unto the nations" (Jeremiah 1:5).

So much illumination came from the revelation received and contemplations made in the dimly lit Liberty Jail. This Missouri dungeon served as Joseph's tutoring temple during months of incarceration, months of preparation for the final five years of his earthly ministry.

Notes

1. For instance, the Testament of Naphtali 2:2–4 (cir. 100 B.C.), fragments of which were found at Qumran, states, "First the potter knows the vessel, how much it is to contain, and bringeth clay accordingly, so also doth the Lord make the body after the likeness of the spirit, and according to the capacity of the body does he implant the spirit." (As Blake Ostler observed in an October 14, 1985 letter to the author, Marc Philonenko, a French scholar, said the Testament of Naphtali clearly teaches "the doctrine of the pre-existence of the soul" [Marc Philonenko, Les Interpolations Chretiennès des Testaments des Douze Patriarches, Paris:1960, p. 39].)

2. Or, in the Greek, foreordained.

3. See note 2.

4. For a discussion concerning the teachings about the premortal existence of man as compared in Hellenic, Judaic, and LDS sources, see *Reflections on Mormonism: Judaeo-Christian Parallels* (Provo, Utah: Religious Studies Center, Brigham Young University, 1978), pp. 13–35.

5. As for apocryphal (and, presumably, pseudepigraphic) writings, the Lord has counseled, "There are many things contained therein that are true, . . . many things . . . that are not . . . ; the Spirit manifesteth truth; and whoso is enlightened by the Spirit shall obtain benefit therefrom." (D&C 91:1–5.) An example of pseudepigraphic literature is the Slavonic Enoch: "The souls of mankind, however many of them are born and the places prepared for them to eternity; for all souls are prepared to eternity, before the foundation of the world" (2 Enoch 23:4–5).

6. Origen wrote of the foreordination of Jacob, reasoning that God would be unjust to choose Jacob over Esau from birth unless that choice was related to their previous existence (*De Principiis* III, i.20).

CHAPTER 5

"Organized Before the World Was" Abraham 3:22

*T*he doctrine of premortality can strengthen and reassure us in all circumstances, as it doubtless did Joseph when, at sunset, he peeked through the grates of "this lonesome prison." Whether we are confronted by confinement or vastness, the doctrine succors us. Indeed, while gazing at the heavens on a starlit night the thoughtful soul can have an inkling, though on a very small scale, of how Moses must have felt after the spectacular but humbling panorama the Lord presented to him regarding this one particular planet: "And it came to pass that it was for the space of many hours before Moses did again receive his natural strength like unto man; and he said unto himself: Now, for this cause I know that man is nothing, which thing I never had supposed" (Moses 1:10).

Overwhelmed by both the vastness of "the world upon which he was created" as well as the demographic detail—"all the children of men which are, and which were created"—Moses "greatly marveled and wondered." What he saw confirmed man's worth in the sight of God even though, comparatively speaking, a meek man may feel he is "nothing" (see Mosiah 4:5). In God's plans, man, as God's child, is as "everything" to him. Our loving, redeeming Father has so said, declaring to an overwhelmed and meek Moses: "For behold, this is my work and my glory—to bring to pass the immortality and eternal life of man" (Moses 1:39).

This declaration is consistent with other declarations from the Lord and his prophets:

> For thus saith the Lord that created the heavens; God himself that formed the earth and made it; he hath established it, he created it not in vain, he formed it to be inhabited: I am the Lord; and there is none else (Isaiah 45:18).

> Behold, the Lord hath created the earth that it should be inhabited; and he hath created his children that they should possess it (1 Nephi 17:36).

> He doeth not anything save it be for the benefit of the world; for he loveth the world (2 Nephi 26:24).

> For we saw him, even on the right hand of God; and we heard the voice bearing record that he is the Only Begotten of the Father—
> That by him, and through him, and of him, the worlds are and were created, and the inhabitants thereof are begotten sons and daughters unto God. (D&C 76:23–24.)

The truth about man's premortal existence thus can cradle us amid the vastness and the otherwise inexplicableness of space, reassuring us of man's worth and of God's overseership. As we encounter the "what" of space, the plan of salvation gives to us the "why." If it were not so we might myopically conclude that "all flesh is grass" (Isaiah 40:6), ultimately as well as proximately. Isaiah's words, however, pertain not to man's *worthlessness* but to the *transitoriness* of this second estate. It is the briefest of our estates, like unto the "small moment" twice emphasized by the Lord to Joseph in the prison-temple.

This powerful, plain doctrine of premortality contains nourishment, both explicit and implicit, to sustain us during our afflictions and adversities—which, comparatively, "shall be but a small moment" (D&C 121:7). Indeed, in the words of the hymn, we should let this doctrine "as the dew from heaven distilling" revive us, "thus fulfilling / What [God's] providence intends" (*Hymns* [new edition], no. 149).

As pertains to this expansive doctrine, we should do what King Benjamin advised—"Believe that man doth not comprehend all the things which the Lord can comprehend" (see Mosiah 4:9–10). If necessary, we should even be willing to say, "Lord, . . . help thou my unbelief" (Mark 9:24).

The acceptance of the reality that we are in the Lord's hands is only a recognition that we have never really been anywhere else.

As already observed, this doctrine of premortality is not, however, an excusing or relaxing doctrine. For each of us there are choices to be made, chores to be done, adversities and ironies to be experienced, time to be well spent, and talents and gifts to be well employed. Because we were chosen "there and then" surely does not mean that we can relax "here and now." Having been chosen and having been prepared "then," the work remains to be done by us "now."

It was surely hard work for foreordained Joseph, through whom this doctrine was revealed, but, as promised, Joseph liked to do the work to which he had been called "before the world was."

In fact, adequacy in the first estate may have merely insured a stern second estate with many duties and no immunities. Additional schooling by suffering (along with the suffering common to man which is caused by our own mistakes and sins) appears to be the pattern for the Lord's most apt pupils (see Mosiah 3:19; 1 Peter 4:19).

How earnestly the adversary has striven to keep the doctrines of the premortal existence of man and the reality of the resurrection from coming generally within man's circle of awareness, let alone conviction! When people are thus deprived, this creates a one-dimensional man. If created *ex nihilo*, man did not really exist before; this false doctrine, Joseph said at the 1844 Follett funeral, "lessens man" (*Words*, p. 359).

Denying the doctrine of the premortal existence of man shrinks man's perspective. He begins to think, mistakenly, that this life is all there is; that the insignificant "me" of a tiny "now" is not only all there is, but all there ever was. The adversary is quick to use the *"what if"* there is no purpose to life in order to induce some to act *"as if"* such were the case. The resultant misbehavior only deepens the despair (see Moroni 10:22).

Naturally, such a view tends to be accompanied by a diminished belief or a pronounced unbelief in the resurrection and a perpetuation of personality, which pushes a person's hope for the future down to nil. This "no-answer" attitude equates with a "no-answerability" concept that too often leads to the "eat, drink, and be merry" outlook. Thus one-dimensional mortality relentlessly promotes a one-dimensional morality!

The coming forth (through "a choice seer") of the "other books" of scripture, however, makes possible the confounding of the false doctrine of *ex nihilo* man—man created from nothing. More than anyone else in modern times, the "choice seer" did battle with this heresy that became orthodoxy, using the reality of our premortality as his sword. More than we as Church members yet appreciate, this precious truth frees us from the dichotomy of the Creator-creature and from the awful challenge of explaining evil in a mankind created *ex nihilo!* With the truth about our identity comes clarity as to our accountability.

Utilizing full gospel perspective man soon begins to see how everlasting life is. Though very imperfectly, he can then begin to see how purposeful this life is and how bright the future can be. On the other hand, without the full doctrine of the plan of salvation and premortal existence, not only is one's view of life affected but one's view of the universe is shrunken.

Just as the restored gospel expands our understanding of things, secularism shrinks them. It is so easy for one-dimensional man with a one-dimensional view of the world to focus intensively on the cares of this world and to yield to the appetites of this world and of this moment.

Given all the disapprovals of past synods and councils, the doctrine of premortal existence is demonstrably not one that could have been reestablished by backward reasoning or research. It could only have come through modern revelation and restoration. Though the doctrine does not abuse logic, it is more than logic alone can fully support. It rests upon the certitude and direction which can come only from divine revelation and affirmation, which is precisely what occurred.

As is so often the case, these powerful truths must rest awhile upon the mind and upon the soul. They must ripen before they begin to nourish our individual comprehension, and certainly before they provoke our individual articulation. It seems to have been so for Joseph.

Chronologically, as already noted, Joseph Smith would have first encountered this doctrine when he was translating the great bulk of the Book of Mormon. (April–June, 1829.) Whether he then merely intellectually noted the doctrine, amid the relentless pressures of a highly compressed work of translation, we do not know.

Joseph's incomplete but inspired translation of the Bible brought about, as earlier indicated, the revelation we know as the book of Moses. This would have heightened the Prophet's awareness of other worlds, God's plan for man, and, significantly, the creation of all things spiritually before they were naturally on the earth. Even so, Joseph did not often cite the relevant biblical passages pertaining to premortality, as he sometimes did with regard to other key doctrines—such as the nature of God.

Liberty Jail seems to have hastened the process of the Prophet's "going public" with this doctrine. His epistle from the prison-temple to the Church in March, 1839, urged Church leaders and members alike to improve, especially in view of their having been "called and chosen . . . before the foundation of the world." Moreover, Joseph was told in the prison-temple about a "Council of the Eternal God of all other Gods" before the world was (*Writings*, pp. 397, 398). The curtains were being parted ever wider.

The book of Abraham came still later, being published in 1842. It gave immense illumination: "If there be two spirits, and one shall be more intelligent than the other, yet these two spirits, notwithstanding one is more intelligent than the other, have no beginning; they existed before, they shall have no end, they shall exist after, for they are gnolaum, or eternal" (Abraham 3:18).

While the Book of Mormon gave us "precious" information about our premortal existence, it was not given there in overwhelming abundance. This is attested to by the statement of Elder Orson Pratt about the unfolding of this vital doctrine: "Joseph Smith . . . was commanded to translate the Bible by inspiration. . . . This same doctrine [premortal existence] is inculcated in some small degree in the Book of Mormon. However, I do not think that I should have ever discerned it in that book had it not been for the new translation of the Scriptures [Bible], . . .

throwing so much light and information on the subject." (*Journal of Discourses*, 15:249.)

Nor was this doctrine "in the air" in America. All of which makes its coming in its fulness and uniqueness stunning to contemplate.

All we have mentioned on this subject except the book of Abraham came very early in Joseph's ministry. Yet there is an apparent "gap" of six years before the Prophet began to speak or write publicly of the doctrine of premortal existence. With his first recorded public utterance in writing in the March 1839 epistle, his first mention in public speaking was in early August 1839, not long after his Liberty Jail experience.

Willard Richards recorded these words of Joseph Smith:

> The spirit of man is not a created being; it existed from eternity and will exist to eternity. Anything created cannot be eternal; and earth, water, etc.—all these had their existence in an elementary state from eternity. Our Savior speaks of children and says their angels always stand before my Father.
> The Father called all spirits before him at the creation of man and organized them. (*Words*, p. 9.)

The Prophet held forth on this important doctrine on a number of later occasions, according to those who kept some record of his sermons. Several times he spoke about things having been instituted prior to "the foundation of this earth" or noted that "the morning stars sang together [and] the Sons of God shouted for joy" (*Words*, pp. 38–39). Periodic discussions of premortal existence continued thereafter: "At the first organization in heaven we were all present and saw the Savior chosen and appointed, and the plan of salvation made and we sanctioned it" (*Words*, p. 60).

The most remarkable example of Joseph's having developed this doctrine more fully later in his ministry occurs in his King Follett sermon given to ten thousand people, perhaps more, on April 7, 1844[1] (*Words*, pp. 340–62). The latest and most complete study of this special sermon is that of Donald Q. Cannon and Larry E. Dahl, published by Brigham Young University's Religious Studies Center.

In this sermon the Prophet spoke of our mortal existence in the context of our being spirit children of our Father in Heaven. Consistent with the May 1833 revelation (section 93), Joseph described the existence of intelligence even before our spirit birth.[2] "Intelligence is eternal and it is self-existing. . . . God has made provision for every spirit in the eternal world." (*Words*, p. 346.)

A few weeks later the Prophet noted that

> Brother Joseph Smith was chosen for the last dispensation or seventh dispensation. [At] the time the grand council set in heaven to organize this world Joseph was chosen for the last and greatest prophet to lay the foundation of God's work of the seventh dispensation. (*Words*, p. 370.)

> At the general and grand council of heaven, all those to whom a dispensation was to be committed, were set apart and ordained at that time, to that calling. The Twelve also as witnesses were ordained. (*Words*, p. 371.)

Joseph's preoccupation with this doctrine can be gauged by these lines: "The great thing for us to know is to comprehend what God did institute before the foundation of the world. Who knows it? It is the constitutional disposition of mankind to set up stakes and set bounds to the works and ways of the Almighty." (*Teachings*, p. 320.)

Also late in his ministry, of course, the Prophet Joseph Smith was heavily involved with teaching and administering the temple endowment and its plain but penetrating truths.

These major doctrines, intertwined, may have been part of what Joseph was so anxious to impart to the Saints—"I never have had opportunity to give them the plan that God has revealed to me," he wrote from the temple-prison (*Writings*, p. 387). Certainly Joseph's urgency about unfolding things is seen in the way he prepared the Twelve subsequently. From January 1844 until his martyrdom, he met with the available members of the Quorum of the Twelve frequently.

The pattern, then, was one in which the impressions and revelations concerning this important doctrine, accumulated over an earlier period of time, appeared in the sermons and writings of

Joseph Smith during the last year or so of his prophetic ministry. Even then, Joseph may have been more ready than the members of the Church were to receive and explore the doctrine, as the reactions, then and since, to the King Follett sermon have amply demonstrated.

Though this doctrine of premortality was not "in the air," it is a doctrine fully consistent with the divine instructions to us to strive to become perfect as are the Father and the Son (Matthew 5:48; 3 Nephi 12:48; 27:27.)

Yet, interesting as the process of its coming forth is, the important thing is that it came forth! Its substance, even more than the process, invites examination and appreciation.

It is a doctrine which brings both unarguable identity and severe accountability to our lives. It underscores the actuality of the brotherhood of man as a result of the actuality of the Fatherhood of God, both as the Father of our spirits and as a loving Father whose plan of salvation for his children is his work and glory; this second or mortal estate is the unfolding which follows the shaping first estate. It is also a doctrine which explains things as they really were, are, and will become.

This is a doctrine, likewise, which reminds us mortals that we do not have all of the data. There are many times when we must withhold judgment and trust God lest we misread, as did Jesus' disciples when they inquired about the man blind from birth and Jesus gave the immortal reply: "Neither hath this man sinned, nor his parents: but that the works of God should be made manifest in him" (see John 9:1–3). Trusting God's plan even in the midst of "all these things" is thus made easier, because he has so declared his purposes, plainly and simply, concerning the proving and tutoring dimensions of mortality.

This precious doctrine also allows for both promises we earlier made to God and promises we were given earlier by him, back beyond time. We begin to understand that certain mortals were especially called and prepared before the foundations of the world were laid. It thus permits us to have a sense of identity, and to allow for blossoming in our individual lives as well as in the general unfolding of the plan of salvation. Thus we can praise God for all that he has done with us and for us. Moreover, though justifiably unimpressed with ourselves now, we can see that a loving and redeeming God has done so much for us, considering what he had to work with.

The precious knowledge which flows from this doctrine also permits us to maintain both a backward and a forward perspective. It gives us, for instance, cause to entertain a hope such as generous Sir Thomas More expressed with regard to his accusers and defamers (see chapter 6). Such perspectives can make us less inclined to rush to judgment, giving us more humility and more trust in God, for we are truly in his hands. Still!

In light of this doctrine developmental discipleship assumes genuine significance, inasmuch as our individual spiritual growth is so vital to our happiness and salvation. These words of King Benjamin take on added meaning: ". . . and becometh as a child, submissive, meek, humble, patient, full of love, willing to submit to all things which the Lord seeth fit to inflict upon him, even as a child doth submit to his father" (Mosiah 3:19; see Alma 13:28).

It is no accident that Alma's words about what we should be in the process of "becoming" (Alma 13:28) follow by a few verses his preaching about the premortal existence.

Thus, for the Christian, individual existence is not only a continuum but also the motivation for seeking a particular developmental outcome. "All these things" which can give us relevant "experience," as the Lord told Joseph in the prison-temple, can be for our "good."

The grand scheme of tutoring has been under way for a very long time. It was in our first estate that we received our "first lessons in the world of spirits and were prepared to come forth in the due time of the Lord" (D&C 138:56).

All of this brings us now to the need to examine a doctrine within a doctrine within a doctrine. Within the plan of salvation is the doctrine of premortal existence; we then encounter the delicate but important doctrine of foreordination.

The doctrine of foreordination is one of the doctrinal roads "least traveled by." Yet it clearly underlines how very long and how perfectly God has loved each of us and known each of us, with our individual needs and capacities. It is so powerful a doctrine, however, that isolated from other doctrines, or mishandled, it can induce false pride, stoke the fires of fatalism, impact adversely upon agency, cause us to focus on status rather than service, and carry us over into the false doctrine of predestination. President Joseph Fielding Smith warned:

> It is very evident from a thorough study of the gospel and the plan of salvation that a conclusion that those who accepted the Savior were predestined to be saved no matter what the nature of their lives must be an error. . . . Surely Paul never intended to convey such a thought. . . . This might have been one of the passages in Paul's teachings which caused Peter to declare that there are in Paul's writings "some things hard to be understood, which they that are unlearned and unstable, wrest as they do also the other scriptures, unto their own destruction." (*Improvement Era*, May 1963, pp. 350–51; see 2 Peter 3:16.)

Paul stressed running life's race the full distance; he did not intend a casual Christianity in which some had won even before the race started.

Yet, though foreordination is a difficult doctrine, it has been given to us by the living God, through living prophets, for a purpose. It can actually increase our understanding of how crucial this mortal second estate is and can further encourage us in humble good works. This precious doctrine can also help us go the second mile, because it indicates that we are doubly called.

In some ways our second estate, in relationship to our first estate, is like agreeing in advance to surgery. Then the anesthetic of forgetfulness settles in upon us. Just as doctors do not deanesthetize a patient in the midst of authorized surgery to ask him, again, if the surgery should be continued, or varied to meet a now-discovered need, so in mortality we are not periodically asked to reaffirm our previous agreement to come here and to submit ourselves to certain experiences. Of our situation, Truman Madsen has said, "Our amnesia is God's anesthesia." And the surgeon stays with us!

Of course, when we mortals try to fully comprehend rather than graciously accept foreordination, the result is finite minds futilely trying to comprehend omniscience. A full understanding is for now impossible. We simply have to trust in what the Lord has told us, realizing that we are not dealing with guarantees from

God but with extra opportunities—and certainly heavier responsibilities. Foreordained Joseph Smith found himself, for instance, in Liberty Jail and finally in Carthage. He was buffeted by the world from the moment he left the Sacred Grove.

If one's responsibilities are in some ways linked to past performance or to past capabilities, it should not surprise us. If the tutoring one receives bears down especially upon what remains to be refined, why should it be otherwise?

The Lord said, "There is a law, irrevocably decreed in heaven before the foundations of this world, upon which all blessings are predicated. And when we obtain any blessing from God, it is by obedience to that law upon which it is predicated." (D&C 130:20–21.) This eternal law prevailed in the first as well as in the second estate. It should not disconcert us, therefore, that the Lord has indicated that before they came here he chose some individuals to carry out certain assignments in mortality, and that these individuals were foreordained or set apart to those assignments.

Foreordination is like any other blessing—it is a conditional bestowal subject to the recipient's faithfulness. Prophecies foreshadow events without determining the outcome, this being made possible by a divine foreseeing of outcomes. So foreordination is a conditional bestowal of a role, a responsibility, or a blessing which likewise foresees but does not fix the outcome. Remember John's sequence—"called, and chosen, and faithful" (Revelation 17:14).

There have been those who have failed or who have been, in one degree or another, treasonous to their trust or callings—people such as David, Solomon, and Judas. God foresaw the fall of David but was not the cause of it. It was David who saw Bathsheba from the balcony and sent for her and who ordered what happened to her husband, Uriah. But neither was God surprised by such a sad development.

Thus foreordination is clearly no excuse for fatalism, or arrogance, or the abuse of agency. It is not, however, a doctrine that can be ignored simply because it is difficult. Indeed, deep inside the hardest doctrines are some of the pearls of greatest price.

The doctrine pertains not only to the foreordination of prophets but also to God's precise assessment beforehand as to each of those who will respond to the words of the Savior and the prophets. From the Savior's own lips came these words: "I am the good shepherd, and know my sheep, and am known of mine" (John 10:14). Similarly he said, "My sheep hear my voice, and I know them, and they follow me" (John 10:27). Further, he declared, "And ye are called to bring to pass the gathering of mine elect; for mine elect hear my voice and harden not their hearts" (D&C 29:7).

This responsiveness could not be gauged without divine fore-knowledge concerning all mortals and their response to the gospel—a foreknowledge so perfect that it leaves the realm of prediction and enters the realm of prophecy.

It does no violence even to our frail human logic to observe that there cannot be a grand plan of salvation for all mankind unless there is also a plan for each individual. The salvational sum will reflect all its parts.

As part of his infinite foreknowledge, for example, the Lord would need to have perfect comprehension of all the military and political developments in the Middle East for all time. Some of these are unfolding only now, bringing to pass a latter-day con-dition in which Jerusalem, as Zechariah foretold, will be a "cup of trembling," a "burdensome stone for all people." "All nations" will be gathered "against Jerusalem to battle." (Zechariah 12:2, 3; 14:2.)

It should not surprise us that the Lord, who set bounds and habitations before the world was (see Acts 17:26; Deuteronomy 32:8), would know centuries before the event how much money Judas would receive—thirty pieces of silver—at the time he betrayed the Savior (Matthew 26:15, Matthew 27:3, Zechariah 11:12). Or that the Lord would watch over and encourage his prophet in a Missouri jail.

We are permitted at times, through a process we call inspira-tion and revelation, to access that divine databank—the knowl-edge of God—for the narrow purposes at hand. No wonder that experience is so unforgettable!

There are clearly cases of individuals with special limitations in life, conditions we mortals cannot now fully fathom. For all we now know, the seeming limitations may have been an agreed-upon spur to achievement—a developmental equivalent of a "thorn in the flesh." Like him who was "blind from birth," some come to bring glory to God (John 9:1–3). Some are spiritual pioneers in developing nations who are called by revelation in the midst of environmental deprivation.

We must be exceedingly careful therefore about imputing either wrong causes or wrong rewards to all in such varied circumstances. They too are in the Lord's hands, and he loves them perfectly. Indeed, some of those who have required much waiting upon in this life may well be waited upon again by the rest of us in the next world—but for the highest of reasons! Furthermore, the rickshaw wallah of Calcutta who refuses to beg, who instead runs for ten hours a day in order to help his family barely survive, will carry all of his self-discipline and meekness with him into the next world, bringing it to bear on his greatly enlarged opportunities there.

President Joseph Fielding Smith said: "In regard to the holding of the priesthood in pre-existence, I will say that there was an organization there just as well as an organization here, and men there held authority. Men chosen to positions of trust in the spirit world held priesthood." (Doctrines of Salvation 3:81.)

Surely women, no less than men, were assigned certain mortal roles through some means of fore-designation. Mary was not accidentally the mother of Jesus, or Lucy Mack the mother of the latter-day Joseph. The divine design of our Father is present in the plans for all of his faithful children, regardless of race or gender.

Alma speaks about foreordination with great effectiveness and links it to the foreknowledge of God and, perhaps, even to our previous performance as well as performance here (Alma 13:3–5).

Elder Orson Hyde said of our life in the premortal world, "We understood things better there than we do in this lower world." As to the agreements we made there, he also surmised, "It is not impossible that we signed the articles thereof with our own hands —which articles may be retained in the archives above, to be presented to us when we rise from the dead, and be judged out of our own mouths, according to that which is written in the books." "The veil is thick between us . . . ," said Elder Hyde, "but our forgetfulnesss cannot alter the facts." (*Journal of Discourses*, 7:314–15.) Hence the degree of detail involved in the covenants and promises participated in at that time may be a more highly customized thing than many of us surmise. Yet on occasion, even with our forgetting, there are inklings. President Joseph F. Smith said:

> But in coming here, we forgot all, that our agency might be free indeed, to choose good or evil, that we might merit the reward of our own choice and conduct. But by the power of the Spirit, in the redemption of Christ, through obedience, we often catch a spark from the awakened memories of the immortal soul, which lights up our whole being as with the glory of our former home. (*Gospel Doctrine*, pp. 13–14.)

It is imperative that we always keep in mind the caveats noted earlier, so that we do not indulge ourselves, or our whims, simply because of the presence of this powerful doctrine of foreordination, for with special opportunities come heavy responsibilities and much greater risks. We can be "called" but behave so as to remain "unchosen"!

Nevertheless the doctrine of foreordination properly understood and humbly pursued can help us immensely in coping with the vicissitudes of life. Otherwise, time can play so many tricks upon us. We should always understand that while God is not surprised, we often are.

Life's episodes may thus take on new meaning. For instance, Simon, a Cyrenian, came into Jerusalem that very day and was pressed into service by Roman soldiers to help carry the cross of Christ (Mark 15:21). Simon's son, Rufus, joined the Church and was so well thought of by the Apostle Paul that the latter mentioned Rufus in his epistle to the Romans, describing him as "chosen in the Lord" (Romans 16:13). Was it, therefore, a mere accident that Simon "who passed by, coming out of the country" was asked to bear the cross of Jesus?

The pattern of proving the chosen pertains to whole peoples, too: "And thou shalt remember all the way which the Lord thy

God led thee these forty years in the wilderness, to humble thee, and to prove thee, to know what was in thine heart, whether thou wouldest keep his commandments, or no" (Deuteronomy 8:2).

Properly humbled and instructed concerning the great privileges that are ours, we can cope with what seem to be very dark days. With true perspective about "things as they really are," we can see in them a great chance to contribute. Churchill, trying to rally his countrymen in an address at Harrow School on October 29, 1941, appealed to them:

> Do not let us speak of darker days; let us speak rather of sterner days. These are not dark days: these are great days—the greatest days our country has ever lived; and we must all thank God that we have been allowed, each of us according to our stations, to play a part in making these days memorable in the history of our race. (*Bartlett's Familiar Quotations*, 14th ed. [Boston: Little, Brown and Company, 1968], p. 923.)

The truth about foreordination also helps us to taste of the other deep wisdom of Alma: he said we ought to be "content with the things which the Lord hath allotted unto" each of us (Alma 29:3). If, indeed, the things allotted to each of us have been divinely customized, then "why should I desire more than to perform the work to which I have been called?" (Alma 29:6.)

So should we regard the dispensation of the fulness of times— even when we face stern challenges and circumstances. "These are great days!" Our hearts need not fail us. We can be equal to our challenges.

For us to seek to wrench ourselves free of our schooling circumstances (as obviously distinguished from that betterment we are to seek) could be to tear ourselves away from carefully matched opportunities. To rant and to rail could be to go against divine wisdom, wisdom in which we may once have concurred before we came here. God knew beforehand each of our coefficients for coping and contributing.

President Henry D. Moyle said: "I believe that we, as fellow workers in the priesthood, might well take to heart the admonition of Alma and be content with that which God has allotted us. We might well be assured that we had something to do with our 'allotment' in our pre-existent state. This would be an additional reason for us to accept our present condition and make the best of it. It is what we agreed to do." (Conference Report, October 1952, p. 71.)

With regard to our individual traits and personalities, obviously genes and environment play a large part. But more important than we now know is the luggage we bring with us from the premortal world. In any case, having been rescued from the false doctrine of *ex nihilo* creation of man, we should be very careful about imputing to God any spiritual deficiencies we may have— especially since it is under his tutelage that we are to overcome these.

What a vastly different view of life the doctrine of foreordination gives to us! Shorn of this perspective, some are puzzled by, indifferent toward, or bitter about life. Neither provincialism nor pessimism permits a person to see himself, life, or the universe as these things "really are" and "as they really will be" (Jacob 4:13).

The disciple too will be puzzled at times. But he persists. Later he rejoices and exclaims over how wonderfully things fit together, realizing only then that—with God—things never were apart.

In some of those precious and personal moments of discovery there will be a sudden surge of recognition of an immortal insight, a doctrinal *déjà vu*. We will sometimes experience a flash from the mirror of memory that urges us forward to a far horizon.

When in situations of stress we wonder if there is any more in us to give, we can be comforted to know that God, who knows our capacity perfectly, placed us here to succeed. No one was foreordained to fail or to be wicked.

When we feel overwhelmed, let us recall the assurance given through Joseph that God, who knows we "cannot bear all things now," will not overprogram us; he will not press upon us more than we can bear (see D&C 50:40).

The doctrine of foreordination is not a doctrine of repose; instead, it is a doctrine for second- and third-milers, and it will draw out of them the last full measure of devotion.

It is a doctrine for the deep believer but it will bring only scorn from the skeptic.

When, as President Joseph F. Smith said, we "catch a spark from the awakened memories of the immortal soul," let us be quietly grateful. When of great truths we can say "I know," that powerful spiritual witness may also carry with it the sense of our having known before. With rediscovery, we are really saying "I know—again!"

Until we know more about what Joseph was told in Liberty Jail about "the Council of the Eternal God of all other gods before this world was" (D&C 121:32), we must be elatedly content with the fact that the council was concerned with us as Heavenly Father's children. It is that, for now, which we need to know—there is a redemptive design and a loving Designer! It is through Joseph Smith that we are given such reassuring answers to those everlastingly important questions.

Precious indeed is the doctrine of our premortal existence, with its discernments as to the testing and developing of the Lord's disciples:

> To him that overcometh will I grant to sit with me in my throne, even as I also overcame, and am set down with my Father in his throne (Revelation 3:21).

For us to overcome requires us to reach that point at which, in words translated by Joseph, there is a "yielding [of our] hearts unto God" (Helaman 3:35).

"Being *called*," therefore, is not always precisely the same as "being *chosen*," and even those "chosen" must still finally qualify as those who are *"faithful"* (see D&C 121:34–35).

Called, chosen, and faithful Joseph Smith, who slept on a "dirty straw" couch in a "lonesome, dark, and dirty" jail in Liberty, was in that sense triply crowned, for he "endured it well."

Notes

1. King Follett, a fellow Vermonter, was imprisoned in Missouri at roughly the same time as Joseph, but in a different jail. Empathetic Joseph worried that the prisoners in Richmond Jail "are much more inhumanly treated

than we are" (*Writings*, p. 419). No doubt the feelings Joseph felt for this "Beloved Brother" "were had in mind" as Joseph gave the funeral sermon which, to this day, bears the name of Joseph's fellow prisoner. The lengthy sermon (over two hours) left Joseph "so worn out that he could speak only a few minutes" on the next day. (*Words*, p. xviii.)

2. As Truman Madsen has written, "The King Follett discourse, for example, which until now has seemed unprecedented, is here shown to be the outcome of earlier teachings. Its brilliance and stature emerge from its combining strands of prior insights of the Prophet into one majestic, comprehensive statement." (*Words*, p. xiii.)

CHAPTER 6

"Endure It Well" D&C 121:8

As the Prophet Joseph Smith was told in the prison-temple, experiencing and enduring are part of the essence of significant spiritual development, the end for which all serious disciples are to strive. The Missouri dungeon provided just such a tutoring mixture of obscurity, adversity, irony, and testimony.

Three times Jesus has told us that we are to seek to become like the Father and like the Savior, an objective not to be reached without obedience in the midst of soul stretching:

> Be ye therefore perfect, even as your Father which is in heaven is perfect (Matthew 5:48).

> Therefore I would that ye should be perfect even as I, or your Father who is in heaven is perfect (3 Nephi 12:48).

> Therefore, what manner of men ought ye to be? Verily I say unto you, even as I am. (3 Nephi 27:27.)

This same pattern was operative anciently, as evidenced by the Lord's allowing some of the heathen nations with their influence to remain in the land of Caanan as Israel's neighbors: "And they were to prove Israel by them, to know whether they would hearken unto the commandments of the Lord, which he commanded their fathers by the hand of Moses" (Judges 3:4).

Some of the soul-stretching experiences are so wrenching that even the best Saints need reassurance during the process: "Know thou, my son, that all these things shall give thee experience, and shall be for thy good" (D&C 122:7). Has the Lord provided similar assurances and such tender tutoring to other prophets in other ages and extremities? We do not know the complete answer on this, but if so, given his varied and significant challenges, Joseph the son of Jacob would surely have qualified.

When one ponders the words of that ancient Joseph concerning the latter-day seer and prophet, "he shall be like unto me" (2 Nephi 3:15), certain similarities are striking, though of varying exactitude.

Initially both had inauspicious beginnings and were unlikely candidates to make the impact they did—whether in ancient Egypt or in modern America.

Both had visions at young and tender ages (see Genesis 37:2–5; Joseph Smith—History 1).

The visions brought both men hatred. Both men knew sibling jealousy or other ill feelings. Ancient Joseph's brothers "envied him" (Genesis 37:7–11). Modern Joseph had to contend with a mercurial brother, William, whom he forgave many times (*History of the Church* 2:353–54).

Both men were falsely accused.

Both Josephs were generous to those who betrayed them. Ancient Joseph was generous to his once-betraying brothers, whom he later saved from starvation (Genesis 43:29–30).

Both men were jailed and knew what it was to be in a "pit" (Genesis 37:23–24).

Both prophesied remarkably of the future of their nations (Genesis 41:29–31; D&C 87).

Both men helped those who shared their imprisonment but later forgot them. With ancient Joseph, it was the chief butler (Genesis 40:21–23); modern Joseph worried over ill Sidney Rigdon, who was freed in January, 1839. The Prophet rejoiced. Three months later, the Prophet inquired "after Elder Rigdon if he has not forgotten us" (*Writings*, p. 399).

Both were "like unto" each other in being amazingly resilient in the midst of adversity, a truly striking quality.

Both knew separation from their families and friends. Ancient and anxious Joseph asked the question of his brothers, "Doth my father yet live?" (Genesis 45:3.) Modern Joseph, during his imprisonment, asked the question, "Doth my friends yet live? If they live, do they remember me?" (*Writings,* p. 409.)

With these and perhaps other similarities, it is no wonder that ancient Joseph wrote foretellingly of modern Joseph, "He shall be like unto me." And, significantly, modern Joseph wrote from Liberty Jail amid afflictions, "I feel like Joseph in Egypt" (*Writings,* p. 409).[1]

For ancient Joseph, adversity and absence from family and home paved the way for his later preservation of the lives of many Egyptians and others (see Genesis 45:5; 50:20). The modern Joseph ended a different form of "famine in the land" (see Amos 8:11–12), becoming the means of bringing spiritual food to millions upon millions!

We are left to wonder how much pondering Joseph Smith, Jr., did with regard to the words in the Book of Mormon which he translated and which forecast his special relationship with ancient Joseph. In any event, the special relationship of the two Josephs was further reinforced by revelation which came to him in 1830 while translating Genesis chapter 50, and by a father's blessing in 1834. Finally, in Liberty Jail in 1839, Joseph wrote of the parallel![2]

Clearly, for us and the prophets to be so prepared and tutored requires a system that features *proving, reproving,* and *improving.* Properly responded to, all these experiences can lead us, attribute by attribute, to become ever more like the Father and the Son. Just as Joseph's successor, Brigham Young, once said of a destination finally reached, "This is the place," so it might be said of God's developmental pattern for mortality, "This is the process."

It is important, however, for us to recognize in all of this that we must first truly desire such spiritual development (see D&C section 4). Like the desire for faith and knowledge, in the matter of spiritual growth we must first desire and then let the desire work within us until we can believe sufficiently to give heedful place for a portion of the Lord's words to operate in our lives (Alma 32:27–28).

Then, as this process of challenge and response unfolds, we must be able to "endure it well" and "valiantly," as the Prophet was told in Liberty Jail, and to see, if necessary, months or even years as merely constituting "a small moment" (D&C 121:7–8, 29; 122:4).

Paul wrote with the same perspective about our afflictions being "but for a moment" and yet that they "worketh for us a far more exceeding and eternal weight of glory" (2 Corinthians 4:17).

Desire, challenge, obedient response, and subsequent development interplay in the life of each serious disciple. So with Abraham: "And said unto him, Get thee out of thy country, and from thy kindred, and come into the land which I shall shew thee." Commanded by the Lord to go to another land, Abraham obeyed: "Then came he out of the land of the Chaldaeans, and dwelt in Charran: and from thence, when his father was dead, he removed him into this land, wherein ye now dwell." (Acts 7:3, 4.)

Yet this direction depended for its fulfillment upon the genuineness of Abraham's desire for greater happiness, greater peace, and greater rest. Abraham realized he was a rightful heir, entitled to be a high priest, so he genuinely sought the blessings of the fathers and the ordination. He desired to administer the blessings of the fathers to others as a true follower of righteousness. (See Abraham 1:1–2.)

Because Abraham really *desired* several outcomes, his discipleship was a serious and obedient discipleship. The rest is superb religious history. Though not told about them, we can be sure that there were plenty of pressing "cares of the world" in which Abraham could have earnestly and sincerely entangled himself. But he chose otherwise because he desired otherwise.

This same process pertains to the development of all disciples. It is not just for the prophets.

Such development usually occurs in a world too busy to notice and too disdainful when it does. Little wonder that obscurity is often the setting and adversity the catalyst!

Historian Dean Jessee has written well[3] of the adversity in the days in Liberty Jail, which, with its window looking into developmental discipleship, tells us much about the crunching moments and the stern stuff of which such challenges are made.

> An eye-witness who saw the prisoners arrive said that Joseph Smith was the last to enter the jail. He "looked at the curious multitude that had gathered . . . lifted his hat and said in a distinct voice,

'Good afternoon, gentlemen,' and disappeared behind the heavy iron door." (Lyman Littlefield, Remin., of LDS, pp. 79–80; quoted in Dean Jessee's manuscript *"Walls, Grates, and Screeking Iron Doors":* *The Prison Experiences of Mormon Leaders in Missouri—1838–1839.*)

Shortly after his call to the Council of the Twelve in 1839, George A. Smith described his visit in company with Brigham Young and Heber C. Kimball:

"We traveled next day to Liberty, and put up at a hotel, waited till victuals were carried in, towards evening to the prisoners, when Judge Tillery and the jailor permitted us to go in and see the prisoners. We were locked in with them for about an hour. Joseph told me of my calling to the Apostleship and enquired how I liked it. I replied I was pleased with the appointment, and would do my best to honor it. He spent most of the time conversing with Brothers Brigham and Heber, and I have always regarded it as a blessing that I had the privilege of being locked up with those who were imprisoned for the Kingdom of heaven's sake, if it was but for an hour." (George Albert Smith Memoirs, pp. 123–125; quoted in the Dean Jessee manuscript.)

As word of the occupants of the prison spread, the place took on some of the aspects of a zoo. Hyrum Smith was exasperated at the curiosity seekers who crowded to see them. "We are often inspected by fools who act as though we were elephants or dromedarys or sea hogs or some monstrous whale or sea serpents. We have never had our teeth examined like an old horse, but expect [to] every day when . . . a new swarm come[s] that have never seen us." (HS Diary, 3.18.1839; quoted in the Dean Jessee manuscript.)

Lyman Wight spoke of the "scanty" rations which he, the Prophet, and others received in Liberty Jail. I have previously noted that what was supplied came frequently by way of leftovers from the jailer's own table, brought "in a basket, on which the chickens had roosted the night before without being cleaned."

Faced with such circumstances, a failure to understand the tutoring, improving, and reproving dimension of this mortal life can cause us to "stumble exceedingly" (1 Nephi 13:34). The absence of such precious and plain perspective can result in resentment toward life and, unlike the response of stout Job, in our "[charging] God foolishly" (Job 1:22).

In "all these things" the importance of having a clear view of reality in order to achieve personal spiritual development cannot be overemphasized.

This journey of deepening discipleship, therefore, is not one step but many. It is the work of this lifetime, and more. Indeed, as already shown, our journey actually began long, long ago.

Irony often joins adversity and obscurity as part of the challenges which go with soul stretching. There are many examples of the interplay of irony and history. Human history's greatest and saddest irony is that a few of the mortal family crucified their perfect King, Jesus Christ: ". . . and there is none other nation on earth that would crucify their God" (2 Nephi 10:3; see Acts 2:36).

There are happy ironies in human affairs, however. Paul—a zealous, legalistic Pharisee devoted to a keen and strict observance of the law of Moses—went through the "mighty change" in his heart and life after being called by the crucified but resurrected Christ. Later Paul gave us the supernal verses on charity (see 1 Corinthians 13). It was Paul, ironically, who spent much of his ministry in striving against the Judaizing of converts to Christianity.

There is yet another irony in Paul's ministry: He was earlier present as a cloak holder at the stoning of Stephen.

Of this episode Sir Thomas More, himself a victim of and witness to an abundance of irony, generously observed just as he was about to be martyred:

> Paul . . . was present, and consented to the death of St. Stephen, and kept their clothes that stoned him to death, and yet be they [Stephen and Paul] now both twain Holy Saints in heaven, and shall continue there friends for ever, so I verily trust and . . . pray, that though your lordships have now here in earth been judges to my condemnation, we may yet hereafter in heaven merrily all meet together, to our everlasting salvation. (Anthony Kenny, *Thomas More* [Oxford University Press, 1983], p. 88.)

Sir Thomas More, as an adviser, had earlier warned Henry VIII:

> "I must put your Highness in remembrance of one thing, and that is this. The Pope, as Your Grace knoweth, is a Prince as you are, and in league with all the other Christian Princes. It may hereafter so fall out that Your Grace and he may vary upon some points of the league, whereupon may grow breach of amity and war between you both. I think it best, therefore, that the place be amended, and his authority more slenderly touched."

"Nay," quoth His Grace, "that shall it not. We are so much bounden unto the See of Rome that we cannot do too much honour to it." (*Thomas More*, p. 51.)

Later on, the Pope excommunicated Henry VIII. More would not endorse Henry's marriage to Anne Boleyn and was beheaded at the order of the same king he had warned not to be too close to the Pope! More, ironically, was made a Catholic saint, having lost his life at the hands of a king who once said he could not do too much to honor the Pope.

One genuinely hopes that at least some of the critics of or the defectors from The Church of Jesus Christ of Latter-day Saints will, with change of heart, one day be able to experience the same happy irony which Paul and Stephen experienced.

There was irony in Liberty Jail: grossly abused by men and a system which exercised unrighteous dominion, Joseph was there schooled in the Lord's refined way of leadership. The two unsuccessful escape efforts preceded the great and emancipating revelations to Joseph. Though told before of his special relationship to ancient Joseph, it was in Liberty that the Prophet first publicly noted it. Though deprived of constitutional rights, Joseph hailed the United States Constitution. Though betrayed by friends who helped put him there, Joseph was counseled to be long-suffering. Though in bad circumstances, Joseph was told it should be for his good.

In any case, part of what must be endured "well" and "valiantly" (D&C 121:8, 29) is irony. Irony is so often like salt in an already painful wound, or like giving vinegar to the thirsty (see Matthew 27:34, 48). But irony, meekly experienced, can stiffen righteous resolve and deepen memory.

Empathy, mercy, and humility can emerge from adversity much enhanced. Joseph himself traced increased feelings of sensitivity to his Liberty Jail experience:

No tongue can tell what inexpressible joy it gives a man to see the face of one who has been a friend, after having been inclosed in the walls of a prison for five months. It seems to me that my heart will always be more tender after this than ever it was before . . . For my part I think I never could have felt as I now do if I had not suffered the wrongs that I have suffered. All things shall work together for good to them that love God. (*Writings*, pp. 386–87.)

Furthermore, according to what was revealed in Liberty Jail, the Restoration was not—and is not—fully finished yet! There is much more to come, as we see in these verses:

> God shall give unto you knowledge . . . that has not been revealed since the world was until now;
>
> Which our forefathers have awaited with anxious expectation to be revealed in the last times, which their minds were pointed to by the angels, as held in reserve for the fulness of their glory;
>
> A time to come in the which nothing shall be withheld, whether there be one God or many gods, they shall be manifest.
>
> All thrones and dominions, principalities and powers, shall be revealed and set forth upon all who have endured valiantly for the gospel of Jesus Christ.
>
> And also, if there be bounds set to the heavens or to the seas, or to the dry land, or to the sun, moon, or stars—
>
> All the times of their revolutions, all the appointed days, months, and years, and all the days of their days, months, and years, and all their glories, laws, and set times, shall be revealed in the days of the dispensation of the fulness of times—
>
> According to that which was ordained in the midst of the Council of the Eternal God of all other gods before this world was, that should be reserved unto the finishing and the end thereof, when every man shall enter into his eternal presence and into his immortal rest. (D&C 121:26–32.)

Our forefathers "awaited with anxious expectation" for these things—to be had only in the very last times. This remarkable array of things yet to come will, of course, include the fulness of the Apostle John's record: "And it shall come to pass, that if you are faithful you shall receive the fulness of the record of John" (D&C 93:18).

But John's record was had once before, and the things being discussed now apparently have *never* been fully revealed, from the beginning of the world.

When the time comes the Lord will "set forth" further things we need to know about "thrones, dominions, principalities, and powers." Will the faithful then know what ancient Abraham earlier knew? Yes, but also more! Some promised knowledge concerns the astro-physical order of the cosmos, its appointed days and years, the set times, glories, and laws that pertain to the sun, the moon, the stars, and the heavens. Perhaps even more important, we will then learn about matters "according to that which was ordained in the midst of the Council of the Eternal God of all other gods" before the world was.

We are enclosed in the midst of effulgent, everlasting meaning.

Therefore, while Liberty Jail had only two small windows out of which Joseph could look when permitted, the widest window in Liberty Jail was that through which the Prophet received a tremendous amount that mattered, including the promises of revelation to come to the Church much later, having been "reserved unto the finishing and the end thereof" (D&C 121:32).

As noted, the grim conditions of Joseph and his fellow prisoners caused them to make two attempts at escape. Both of them failed. The revelations, on the other hand, provided conceptual breakouts which no mortal could prevent, emancipating the Prophet Joseph Smith and his followers from provincialism forever.

Even with and perhaps because of such vistas, the revelations given to jailed Joseph counseled him to be patient. This included being patient about the manner and the season in which the Lord will bring judgment upon those who are the sworn enemies of his work; he will bring his "swift judgment in the season thereof" (D&C 121:24), that season not being always according to the timetable we might desire.

Elsewhere the Lord said that the confounding of the enemies of his work would be done "in mine own due time" (D&C 71:10). Once again, there is the reminder of the importance of patience.

In pondering the expectations which go with being called and chosen, we recognize that "many" are called but "few" are chosen (D&C 121:34). One reason for the distinction between being "called" and being "chosen" is that the latter can understand this next reality: the powers of heaven are accessed and controlled only upon the principles of righteousness (D&C 121:36).

The Lord thus drew a sharp distinction, and this in the midst of the abuse and injustice of Liberty Jail, between those who would use power as it is usually employed: to cover their sins, glorify their pride and ambition, and seek control or dominion over others—and those who would lead as Jesus led.

Still earlier, at Kirtland, a parallel prescription came to Joseph about how the quorums composed of these priesthood holders should make decisions. The same virtues are to operate: "The decisions of these quorums, or either of them, are to be made in all righteousness, in holiness, and lowliness of heart, meekness and long suffering, and in faith, and virtue, and knowledge, temperance, patience, godliness, brotherly kindness and charity; because the promise is, if these things abound in them they shall not be unfruitful in the knowledge of the Lord" (D&C 107:30–31; see 2 Peter 1:8).

Unjustly reproved by Missouri's judicial system, Joseph was given almost clinical counsel on how to redeem those who required reproof:

> Reproving betimes with sharpness, when moved upon by the Holy Ghost; and then showing forth afterwards an increase of love toward him whom thou hast reproved, lest he esteem thee to be his enemy;
>
> That he may know that thy faithfulness is stronger than the cords of death. (D&C 121:43–44.)

This redemptive counsel parallels the outreaching counsel of Paul:

> But speaking the truth in love . . . (Ephesians 4:15).
>
> So that contrariwise ye ought rather to forgive him, and comfort him, lest perhaps such a one should be swallowed up with overmuch sorrow.
>
> Wherefore I beseech you that ye would confirm your love toward him. (2 Corinthians 2:7–8.)

Human agency, of course, when misused, produces much misery, irony, and adversity.

At this historical distance we cannot fully measure the interplay within the Prophet of the revelations given him about man's moral agency, man's premortality, God's mercy, and salvation for the dead.

God, who is perfect in love, is not indifferent to human suffering. Being perfect in his love and mercy, how can he possibly be? We are his spirit children. But God is also deeply, deeply committed to man's freedom of choice. Genuine agency, mis-used, may produce not only happy but harsh consequences. The ripple effects roll like tidal waves throughout all of human history.

Therefore, it is important and helpful to ponder, much more than we do now, how the concepts of premortal existence and salvation for the dead are conjoined. When grown together, they are the means of insuring and demonstrating the mercy and jus-tice of God. Clearly, by itself this tight time frame we call mor-tality does not permit such a balancing.

In the brevity of this experience, many die at birth or very young. This makes the doctrine of the plan of salvation even more significant, because our individual existence is a contin-uum, reaching a point at which there will be ultimate justice and mercy.

Though the revelation comprising what is now section 137 of the Doctrine and Covenants was given to Joseph in 1836, it was accepted by the Church as embodied scripture only in 1980. Apparently the gradual process of recognition and appreciation operates institutionally as well as individually. This section's illuminating verses bear directly upon the assurance of the mercy and justice of God and the diverse human circumstance:

> Thus came the voice of the Lord unto me, saying: All who have died without a knowledge of this gospel, who would have received it if they had been permitted to tarry, shall be heirs of the celestial kingdom of God;
> Also all that shall die henceforth without a knowledge of it, who would have received it with all their hearts, shall be heirs of that kingdom;
> For I, the Lord, will judge all men according to their works, according to the desire of their hearts.
> And I also beheld that all children who die before they arrive at the years of accountability are saved in the celestial kingdom of heaven. (D&C 137:7–10.)

There are demographics, too, to drive this doctrine: of the approximately 70 billion individuals who, up to now, have inhab-ited this planet, probably not more than one percent have really heard the gospel. Today no more than one-tenth of one percent of the world's population are members of the Church. Even so, before the final judgment and resurrection *all* will have had an adequate opportunity to hear the gospel of Jesus Christ. This underscores the mercy of God and the justice of God. (See D&C 1:2.) Infant mortality, which rages in so many parts of the world, is also placed in a reassuring doctrinal context (see D&C 137:10).

Only a few (and these are they who were once privileged of the Lord but who, in mortality, betrayed the Lord) will not receive a kingdom of glory. Though differing dramatically in degree, the end results of the atonement of Jesus Christ include everlasting life in the telestial kingdom, which is still a kingdom of glory. Better still will be the terrestrial kingdom; and, of course, the most prized of all, the celestial kingdom.

Concerning what Paul gave us in several verses (about gradations of salvation), Joseph received and transmitted dozens of verses (see 1 Corinthians 15:40–42; D&C 76).

On one occasion the Prophet Joseph observed, "There are some things in my own bosom that must remain there. If Paul could say 'I knew a man who ascended to the third heaven and saw things unlawful for man to utter,' *I more.*" (*Words*, p. 207.)

Little wonder that the Prophet's mind fastened so tightly upon temple work and salvation for the dead near the end of his ministry. No wonder, either, that a long-suffering God does not always punish swiftly. No wonder, either, given the injustice of the human circumstance and the misuse of human moral agency, that we are counseled to "endure it well" and to view the tribulations through which we pass as being "but a small moment."

Not only is Joseph being told, therefore, to put it all in perspective, but so are we.

Not only were Joseph's days known, but no righteous individual dies an untimely death.

Not only is Joseph being reminded that Jesus descended "below all"; we are being reminded, too, about the power and eloquence of Jesus' example. Our faith in him who so "descended" is necessary in order for us to ascend to where he now is. His was a perfected and earned empathy—earned "according to the flesh."

> And he shall go forth, suffering pains and afflictions and temptations of every kind; and this that the word might be fulfilled which saith he will take upon him the pains and the sicknesses of his people.

And he will take upon him death, that he may loose the bands of death which bind his people; and he will take upon him their infirmities, that his bowels may be filled with mercy, according to the flesh, that he may know according to the flesh how to succor his people according to their infirmities. (Alma 7:11–12.)

What we receive, sometimes only in precious fragments, from Paul and others in holy scripture (see Isaiah 53:4–5; Hebrews 2:18; Matthew 8:17) about how Jesus bore not only our sins but also our infirmities and sicknesses is thus given in greater fulness through Joseph Smith.

We see Joseph's dawning consciousness of both his and others' human frailties. Hence his desire that his people allow for the fact that "our light speeches from time to time, they have nothing to do with the fixed principle of our hearts" (*Writings*, p. 376).

Surely the spirit of generosity which the Prophet pledged from Liberty Jail was present in his redemptive, post–Liberty Jail letter (July 22, 1840) to W. W. Phelps, whose betrayal had helped put Joseph in jail. Phelps wrote to Joseph Smith on June 29, 1840, seeking to regain the fellowship and membership he once had. Joseph's reply is a classic:

> Nauvoo, Hancock County, Illinois
> July 22, 1840
> Dear Brother Phelps:
> I must say that it is with no ordinary feelings I endeavor to write a few lines to you in answer to yours of the 29th ultimo; at the same time I am rejoiced at the privilege granted me. You may in some measure realize what my feelings, as well as Elder Rigdon's and Brother Hyrum's were, when we read your letter—truly our hearts were melted into tenderness and compassion when we ascertained your resolves, etc.
> I can assure you I feel a disposition to act on your case in a manner that will meet the approbation of Jehovah (whose servant I am), and agreeable to the principles of truth and righteousness which have been revealed; and inasmuch as long-suffering, patience, and mercy have ever characterized the dealings of our Heavenly Father towards the humble and penitent, I feel disposed to copy the example and cherish the same principles, [and] by so doing be a savior of my fellow men.
> It is true that we have suffered much in consequence of your behavior—*the cup of gall, already full enough* for mortals to drink,

was indeed *filled* to *overflowing* when you turned against us. One with whom we had oft taken sweet counsel together, and enjoyed many refreshing seasons from the Lord—"had it been an enemy, we could have borne it." In the day that thou stoodest on the other side, in the day when strangers carried away captive his forces, and foreigners entered into his gates, and cast lots upon Far West, even thou wast as one of them; but thou shouldst not have "looked on the day of thy brother, in the day that he became a stranger, neither shouldst thou have spoken proudly in the day of distress." However, the cup has been drunk, the will of our Heavenly Father has been done, and we are yet alive, for which we thank the Lord. And having been delivered from the hands of wicked men by the mercy of our God, we say it is your privilege to be delivered from the power of the adversary, be brought into the liberty of God's dear children, and again take your stand among the Saints of the Most High, and by diligence, humility, and love unfeigned, commend yourself to our God, and your God, and to the Church of Jesus Christ.

Believing your confession to be real, and your repentance genuine, I shall be happy once again to give you the right hand of fellowship, and rejoice over the returning prodigal.

Your letter was read to the Saints last Sunday, and an expression of their feeling was taken, when it was unanimously resolved that W. W. Phelps should be received into fellowship.

"Come on, dear brother, since the war is past,
For friends at first are friends again at last."
Yours as ever,
/s/ Joseph Smith, Jr.
(*Writings*, pp. 472–73.)

After the Prophet Joseph's martyrdom, this talented "prodigal" composed "Praise to the Man" (*Hymns* [new edition], no. 27).

Of even greater testifying significance is the hymn of President John Taylor, "The Seer, the Seer, Joseph the Seer"—especially since its author shared in the explosions and cacophony of Carthage!

In readying himself for what would follow the Missouri experiences, Joseph expressed concern over the need to watch over the Church more closely. From Liberty Jail he wrote of this frustration. In his March 1839 epistle to the Church, he observed that some were in their "evil works of darkness going on leading the minds of the weak and unwary into confusion and distraction" while the presidency of the Church were "ignorant as well as innocent" of that which was going on. Joseph displayed a deep concern for the weak and those less able to bear such vexing confusion and distraction. (*Writings*, p. 380.) Unattended to, he wrote, this pattern had given to some "power to lead the minds of the ignorant and unwary and thereby obtain such influence that when we approached their iniquities the devil gained great advantage"[4] (*Writings*, p. 380).

It may have been only the scribal pattern of transcribing the Prophet's epistle for the Church at Quincy, but the Prophet observed how "finally, all enmity, malice, and hatred and past differences, misunderstandings, and mismanagements be slain victims at the feet of hope, and when the heart is sufficiently contrite, then the voice of inspiration steals along and whispers" (*Writings*, p. 394). Sequentially, there then appeared much of the magnificent revelation we now know as section 121, suggesting the Prophet's own readiness to receive the "voice of inspiration."

Given the tutorial explicitness of the prison-temple, as might be expected the first four recorded sermons given by Joseph after emancipation from Liberty Jail show the influence of that profound experience upon him.

On June 27, 1839, as Joseph spoke about the gift of the Holy Ghost, he stressed how vital the "principle of righteousness" is. The earlier revelation received in Liberty Jail declared that "the powers of heaven cannot be controlled nor handled only upon the principles of righteousness" (D&C 121:36; *Words*, p. 3).

On July 2, 1839, in Brigham Young's dwelling in Montrose, Iowa, in counseling the Twelve, Joseph told them that they should "profit by this important key . . . that in all your trials, troubles, and temptations, afflictions, bonds, imprisonment, and death, see to it that you do not betray heaven, that you do not betray Jesus Christ, that you do not betray your brethren, and that you do not betray the revelations of God, whether in the Bible, the Book of Mormon, or the Doctrine and Covenants, or any of the word of God" (*Words*, pp. 7–8). Again, there is the deep urgency and the fervent testimony regarding scripture and revelation.

Having borne testimony from Liberty Jail that God was true

and Jesus Christ was true and the Book of Mormon was true and the Book of Commandments was true (*Writings*, p. 407), a freed Joseph now reminded the people of these and other things.

On July 7, 1839, a Sunday, in an apparently very brief address, Joseph said, "Remember, Brethren, that if you are imprisoned, Brother Joseph has been imprisoned before you. If you are placed where you can only see your Brethren through the gates of a window while in irons because of the gospel of Jesus Christ, remember, Brother Joseph has been in like circumstances." (*Words*, p. 8.) "All these things" had given Joseph experience, for his good and now the Church's.

Also, at some time before August 8, 1839, Joseph gave a doctrinal address stating that "the spirit of man is not a created being; it existed from eternity and will exist to eternity. Anything created cannot be eternal." (*Words*, p. 9.) Surely this doctrine was among the things which, while in Liberty Jail, Joseph felt a sense of urgency to impart to the Saints along with further information about the order and fulness of the holy priesthood.

In November 1839 Joseph reflected upon and gave an account of his Missouri experience and his perspective during those sufferings: "Death stared me in the face, and . . . my destruction was determined upon, as far as man was concerned; yet, from my first entrance into the camp, I felt an assurance that I, with my brethren and our families, should be delivered. Yes, that still small voice, which has so often whispered consolation to my soul, in the depth of sorrow and distress, bade me be of good cheer, and promised deliverance, which gave me great comfort." (*Writings*, p. 443.)

Furthermore, Joseph observed how trials can work together for our good and prepare us "for the society of those who have come up out of great tribulation . . . ; remember the words of the Savior, 'The servant is not above his Lord, if they have persecuted me, they will persecute you also.' . . . Afflictions, persecutions, imprisonments and deaths, we must expect." (*Writings*, p. 444.) A prepared Joseph was, like his Master, striving to prepare his followers for what lay ahead.

When the jailed Joseph was instructed, "Hold on thy way" (D&C 122:9), this counsel meant holding not only onto the iron rod but also to the Christian virtues under development within him. The crisis was no time, for instance, for Joseph to become like his captors—impatient, merciless, and cruel. The events during and after Missouri showed Joseph's determination to stay the course.

Joseph's sense of his impending martyrdom, for instance, was expressed several times, but it is especially significant that it did not contain bitterness. His loyalty to the standard that was the United States Constitution would remain with him, as in this instance: "If I lose my life in a good cause, I am will[ing] to be sacrificed on the altar of virtue, righteousness, and truth in maintaining the laws and Constitution of the United States if need be for the general good of mankind" (*Words*, p. 320).

For all of us, to "hold on" includes, therefore, holding on not only to our beliefs but also to our proven and tested patterns of behavior and Christian virtues under cultivation, and seeking to deepen even further their development. Endurance is continuance in striving for spiritual improvement, outlasting while becoming.

The time may come when the place that was Liberty Jail will be appropriately honored—not only for what it was and what it symbolized for Joseph but also for what it can teach all of us about our own discipleship, as we, in our time and turn, seek to "endure it well."

God's "pavilion" (which understandably seemed to Joseph for a brief, agonizing moment, to be out of range) was not an unreachable, far pavilion. A loving Lord quickly responded to Joseph's pleas and did so in a tender sunburst of celestial communication (see D&C 121:1–8).

The soul-weaving which occurred in Joseph, including that during his sojourn in jail, makes germane these lines by an unidentified author:

My life is but a weaving, between my God and me,
I do not choose the colors, He worketh steadily.
Oftimes He weaveth sorrow, and I, in foolish pride,
Forget He sees the upper, and I the underside.

Not till the loom is silent, and the shuttles cease to fly,
Will God unroll the canvas and explain the reason why
The dark threads are as needful in the Weaver's skillful hand
As the threads of gold and silver in the pattern He has planned.

God saw the upper side, while fools mock Joseph's weaknesses—the underside.

As the ends of the earth inquire after his name, they will come to contemplate the full tapestry of Joseph's life. In this tapestry the strands and threads from the prison-temple will be prominently and resplendently represented.

Notes

1. Only after completing this manuscript did the author read Joseph Fielding McConkie's *Gospel Symbolism* (Salt Lake City: Bookcraft, 1985), which (in pp. 38–43) provides a different treatment of the parallels.

2. Not to be neglected, either, are parallels with Paul which Joseph Smith also noted: Paul experienced much "in stripes, in imprisonments, in tumults, in labours, in watchings, in fastings" (2 Corinthians 6:5). Paul surely knew what it was to be beaten, to be "in perils by mine own country men . . . in the wilderness . . . among false brethren; in weariness and painfulness . . . in hunger . . . in cold," during which, like Joseph, he still had "the care of all the churches" (2 Corinthians 11:24–28).

3. These three quotations from Dean Jessee's unpublished manuscript are used with his generous permission.

4. Joseph's reluctance to recognize betrayal drew comment from his biographer, Elder B. H. Roberts. Elder Roberts observed that the Prophet Joseph, in his generosity, sometimes had "a too great tenacity in friendship for men he had once taken into his confidence after they had been proven unworthy of that friendship" (*Comprehensive History*, 2:358).

CHAPTER 7

"The Ends of the Earth Shall Inquire After Thy Name" D&C 122:1

Today's Church members, all of us, would do well to examine the significant but soul-stretching beginning days of the Church for general perspective but also for indicators as to some things which may likewise stretch us in the unpeaceful, latter days. Though we must be ever careful about allowing for differences in scale and circumstance, there are major lessons for us.

Joseph, as a revelator, received more than he could at first fully understand. Life's experiences and the Lord's counseling further illuminated these truths for him. In fact, Joseph observed that "time and experience" are needed to learn some things. If time and experience are involved, then there is a corresponding need for us to have patience and faith; first, patience to cope with the expanse of time over which some learning occurs; second, faith as evidence of God's unseen purposes to help us pass meekly through the relevant experiences. Is this not the reality which Joseph Smith earlier translated? "Nevertheless the Lord seeth fit to chasten his people; yea, he trieth their patience and their faith" (Mosiah 23:21).

In addition to time and experience, however, solemn searching and contemplating in communicating with God are necessary to find out and to understand the deep things of God. Just as "time and experience" bring about learning, so does searching and trying.

And now, behold, because ye have tried the experiment, . . .
ye must needs know that the seed is good.

And now, behold, is your knowledge perfect? Yea, your knowledge is perfect in that thing, and your faith is dormant; and this
because you know. (Alma 32:33–34.)

If any man will do his will, he shall know of the doctrine,
whether it be of God, or whether I speak of myself (John 7:17).

It is, wrote Jacob and Paul, the Spirit which aids our search:
"for the Spirit . . . speaketh of things as they really are, and of
things as they really will be" (Jacob 4:13; see also 1 Corinthians
2:10). The interplay of time, experience, searching, thinking, pondering, trying, and communicating with God is facilitated by the
Holy Spirit. The scriptures provide a superb way to induce this
interplay, if we will but "feast upon the words of Christ; for
behold, the words of Christ will tell you all things what ye should
do" (2 Nephi 32:3).

So postured, we can then learn from our experiences. Joseph
later spoke of his Missouri experience, counseling the Saints,
"After your tribulations, if you do these things, and exercise
fervent prayer and faith in the sight of God . . . , he shall give
unto you knowledge" (*Writings*, p. 397).

Peter wrote that patience—in part, no doubt, in adversity—
combined with other virtues could produce a special yield:

For if these things be in you, and abound, they make you that
ye shall neither be barren nor unfruitful in the knowledge of our
Lord Jesus Christ (2 Peter 1:8).

But the God of all grace, . . . after that ye have suffered a while,
make you perfect, stablish, strengthen, settle you (1 Peter 5:10).

It is in this setting of managed adversity with our virtues in
evidence that the Lord will keep his promise to pour further
knowledge upon the heads of the Latter-day Saints, individually
and collectively (D&C 121:33).

Virtue is crucial. There is little or no spiritual progress when
individuals, in the words of President Marion G. Romney, "try to
serve the Lord without offending the devil" (*Ensign*, October
1983, p. 6).

Thus we see how experiences illuminate principles, and principles illuminate experiences.

Given the reality of this process, how could our learning be other than "line upon line," experience upon experience, and understanding upon understanding?

Gradual unfolding is seen even in the brightest and the best. Mormon, for instance, puzzled over the actual condition of a translated being: "It did seem unto them like a transfiguration of them." "Whether they were mortal or immortal, from the day of their transfiguration, I know not." Then, "Since I wrote, I have inquired of the Lord, and he hath made it manifest unto me. . . ." (3 Nephi 28:15, 17, 37.) This unfolding of understanding occurred even as Mormon, at one point, had seen the three Nephites and they had ministered to him (v. 26).

As the Prophet Joseph deepened his discipleship he then was in a position to have his understanding expanded under the direction of Heavenly Father. One of the great things we can learn, then, is that the process is always essentially the same for everybody. There are no shortcuts.

If in the midst of "all these things" Joseph came gradually to appreciate some of the deep doctrines which had come through him—whether by translation or revelation—why should we be surprised?

How many times did Jesus tell the original Apostles of the impending resurrection? (See Mark 9:31–32; 16:14; Luke 9:44–45; 18:33–34; 24:25, 41.) Yet only later, after tutoring experiences, did such things dawn on the original Twelve: "These things understood not his disciples at the first: but when Jesus was glorified, then remembered they that these things were written of him, and that they had done these things unto him" (John 12:16).

If the original Twelve at first could not manage what Jesus meant by being about his Father's business (see Luke 2:49–50), or all his declarations of Messiahship (see John 8:25–27), or his parable about his shepherdship and the scattered fold (John 10:6) —why should not Joseph require tutoring time on the subjects of our premortal existence, the plan of salvation, and the nature of God?

In contrast, those who "will not search" or who will not understand the things of God (2 Nephi 32:7), or who "willingly are ignorant" (2 Peter 3:5) will view no stretching vistas. They will ignore the crucial insights called forth by the interplay of revelation and introspection such as Joseph had in the prison-temple.

Others, like the Amulek of his earlier years, will even find that their past spiritual experiences are lost, as they become busy with the pressing cares of the world. Thus preoccupied, the unlearning are "called many times and [they will] not hear" (Alma 10:6).

The manner in which Joseph maintained his felicity in the midst of the adversity, obscurity, and irony of Liberty Jail is impressive indeed. If he had not done so, if he had not followed counsel—"all these things shall give thee experience and shall be for thy good," "endure it well," "hold on the way," and "but a small moment"—there perhaps would not have been an outcome in which "the ends of the earth shall inquire after thy name" (D&C 122:1).

"All these things" included false charges, a biased judicial and political system. Yet Joseph was "of good cheer" and supported the "glorious standard" of the United States Constitution. Clearly the 1833 revelations to Joseph concerning the Constitution's origins and importance were reverenced in the Prophet's expression from jail (see D&C sections 98, 101).

Joseph's being "of good cheer" is all the more commendable in view of the Lord's warning imagery: "Thine enemies prowl around thee" (D&C 122:6); the "very jaws of hell" seemed to gape at him (D&C 122:7). If hell has its own halitosis, Joseph could tell us!

Nor should we forget that the Lord told suffering Joseph Smith in Liberty Jail that hell would "rage" against him (D&C 122:1). *Rage* is not a mild word, and not all the raging against Joseph occurred then. Moreover, "fools shall have [Joseph] in derision" (D&C 122:1). In our day fresh deluges of derision are likely to flow periodically.

The Prophet was warned that there would be those who would lift up their heels against the Lord's anointed, crying that they had sinned when they had not sinned, and such critics would swear falsely (D&C 121:16–20). There is still another lesson which is applicable in our time and is to be distinguished from observing the process of spiritual growth in others. On this lesson, the episode involving Thomas B. Marsh is very instructive. He let a dispute over milk cause him to focus, jealously rather than mercifully, on some minor imperfections in the Prophet Joseph Smith, which finally led to his disaffection and excommunication. Lorenzo Snow, on the other hand, said that while he too had noticed some minor imperfections in the Prophet, he was grateful that the Lord could use Joseph Smith for so very significant a work; and that thus there might be some hope for him, Lorenzo Snow. Indeed, there was hope for President Snow, who viewed others graciously and charitably as if through the "windows of heaven." Indeed, there is hope for all of us if we will let the Lord work with us in our weaknesses.

From the writings of Joseph Smith in Liberty Jail we should ponder other instructive observations, such as the periodic relevance of the following: "Those who bear false witness against us do seem to have a great triumph over us for the present" (*Writings*, p. 375).

Joseph was like a predecessor prophet, Elisha, who was in the grip of a similar circumstance in the sense of its being outwardly hopeless. Even so, Elisha counseled, "Fear not: for they that be with us are more than they that be with them" (2 Kings 6:16). Joseph Smith knew what Elisha knew. So must we.

Joseph wrote echoing Isaiah, "We have spoken words and men have made us offenders" (*Writings*, p. 376; see 2 Nephi 27:32; Isaiah 29:21.) The last episode of this kind has yet to occur.

Joseph saw parallels with John: "they hate us . . . because of the testimony of Jesus Christ" (*Writings*, p. 377; see Revelation 1:9; 6:9; 12:17). This will yet occur, again and again, in the present dispensation.

Joseph's enemies were in some respects less troublesome than former friends. "Mormon dissenters are running through the world and are spreading various foul and libelous reports against us thinking thereby to gain the friendship of the world . . . ; they [the world] make a tool of these fellows . . . and after that they hate them worse than they do us" (*Writings*, p. 379; see also D&C 121:20).

Yet the Prophet was assured that the people of the Church

would never be turned against him by the testimony of traitors (D&C 122:3). Nevertheless, traitors would have sufficient influence to cast him into trouble (D&C 122:4).

Perhaps those now in watchcare roles in the kingdom can learn from Joseph in yet another way. Again, from Liberty Jail: "Your humble servant or servants intend from henceforth to [disapprove] everything that is not in accordance with the fulness of the gospel of Jesus Christ. . . . They will not hold their peace as in times past when they see iniquity beginning to rear its head for fear of traitors or the consequences that shall flow by reproving those who . . . seek to destroy the flock." (*Writings*, pp. 405–6.) Earlier identification and quiet redemptive remonstration are to be preferred to delayed, embittering, public showdowns.

This vow did not mean, however, that the Prophet intended to be less merciful than before. Perhaps he was even more merciful. His redemptive, eloquent letter to W. W. Phelps, quoted previously, is the epitome of a merciful and forgiving spirit.

Like the prophet Samuel, Joseph was often required to perform unpleasant tasks from which he was not to shrink. Having done a disagreeable duty, "Samuel grew, and the Lord was with him, and did let none of his words fall to the ground" (1 Samuel 3:19; see 1 Samuel 2:26; also Luke 2:52).

If Joseph was earlier hesitant to set the Church in order because of concern for how such watchcare would be received, at this distance we cannot confirm it. For us in our time it is not an easy thing for most of us to please the Lord first and mortals next. Aging Eli, an extreme example, was aware that his sons were debauched. He asked them, "Why do ye such things?" but his earlier neglect of his sons' wrongdoings made his later rebuke of them too mild to be effective. So disposed over time, "the sons of Eli . . . knew not the Lord." Moreover, their sensuous life-style caused other of the Lord's "people to transgress."

A prophet came to Eli with the Lord's complaint that Eli "honourest thy sons above me." He had subordinated deference to divinity to deference to family. (See 1 Samuel 2:12–29.)

Some things the adversary inflicted upon the Church in its beginning days may occur again as human affairs enter the winding-up stage in preparation for the second coming of the Savior. The Apostle John, who was permitted to see not only his own time but our time, spoke of the adversary's sense of urgency: "he knoweth that he hath but a short time" (Revelation 12:12).

Peter's words were not overly dramatic when he described the adversary as a "roaring lion" (1 Peter 5:8). The current bellicosity with which the adversary challenges things once sacred suggests he is not merely clearing his throat. After all, he "spreadeth his dominions" (D&C 82:5) and uses barrages of "fiery darts." What are we to do?

These words came as translation through Joseph:

> And I said unto them that it was the word of God; and whoso would hearken unto the word of God, and would hold fast unto it, they would never perish; neither could the temptations and the fiery darts of the adversary overpower them unto blindness, to lead them away to destruction (1 Nephi 15:24).

> Yet you should have been faithful; and he would have extended his arm and supported you against all the fiery darts of the adversary; and he would have been with you in every time of trouble (D&C 3:8).

The Pauline prescription is parallel:

> Praying always with all prayer and supplication in the Spirit, and watching thereunto with all perseverance and supplication for all saints (Ephesians 6:18; see also D&C 27:17).

Helaman, too, wrote of the "whirlwind" in the midst of which are the devil's sharp shafts (Helaman 5:12).

In such inclement and dark "weather," holding fast to the rod of iron (or the word of God—1 Nephi 15:23–24) and having oil in our lamps, rather than complaining of the darkness, is the way.

We should not be surprised, therefore, as such challenges emerge in our time and in our lives. We will likely have opportunities, again and again, to ponder the comforting and consoling words of the Lord to the Prophet Joseph Smith in Liberty Jail, "My son, peace be unto thy soul" (D&C 121:7). Not that the afflictions will thereby be lessened. Surely of all the generations who have ever lived, those who live in the dispensation of the fulness of times cannot expect to be exempt from chastisement and trial (see Mosiah 23:21).

Even when one is steadfast in the midst of "all of these things," there is often an accompanying sorrow. This occurs when those about us, whom we love, fall, defect, or slacken in their faith. This too was something the Prophet Joseph learned to cope with, though the betrayals from inside and the loss of the one-time faithful wrenched his heart more than we can measure.

Whether as leaders, neighbors, or parents, we all have moments when we see others pursuing courses which will produce misery for them and theirs. We should love, remonstrate, and exemplify to the degree we can. But when we have done all we can, it is sometimes to no avail. We are then thrown back, and sometimes none too gently, on the rock of reality: this life is a probationary estate concerning which the Lord has said to us all, "nevertheless, thou mayest choose for thyself" (Moses 3:17).

Moral agency in the face of difficult choices was not for Adam and Eve alone (Moses 7:32; D&C 101:78). There are blessings if we choose aright and penalties if we choose wrongly. Therefore, attempting to stand between friends and the consequences of their wrong choices is not realistic; it is not nearly as useful as being lovingly at their sides before and when choices are being made. Men and women really are "free to choose" (2 Nephi 2:27), and we cannot and should not try to have it otherwise.

Do we always know, however, what consequences will flow from certain decisions? Many times, not. Part of living consists of learning, personally and vicariously, what actions produce what consequences. When we govern ourselves by correct principles, we also govern our consequences.

As men "act according to their wills" (Alma 12:31), there are consequences, good and bad. Part of maturing spiritually is to realize this. One of the great virtues of meekness is making allowance for the fact that God does know best. Trusting him and trusting his principles is an act of high intelligence.

Even so, did the one-third of the hosts of heaven know back *then* all that would later flow from their rebellion? Likely not. But there would have been warning words, "plainly manifest," though they could neither feel in advance nor experience anticipatory anguish. But they were unwilling to trust Father.

> Behold, here is the agency of man, and here is the condemnation of man; because that which was from the beginning is plainly manifest unto them, and they receive not the light (D&C 93:31).

So of the process called the plan of salvation, and of the executing Name thereof, it is correctly said, "there is none other way" (2 Nephi 9:41; Mosiah 3:17; D&C 18:23).

When we see someone striding towards a cliff or the unpleasant consequences of his actions, what are we to do? Joseph said it —move early as the first challenge appears; do early on what is right, without worrying unduly. And what is the manner of reproof, if such is needed?

> Reproving betimes with sharpness, when moved upon by the Holy Ghost; and then showing forth afterwards an increase of love toward him whom thou hast reproved, lest he esteem thee to be his enemy;
>
> That he may know that thy faithfulness is stronger than the cords of death. (D&C 121:43–44.)

Tough love is doing all one can, risking being misunderstood in the process, yet finally accepting that others are meant to be "free to choose." Tough love never quits; it is unconditional. But neither is it unaware of Lehi's "trembling parent" (2 Nephi 1:14).

We are to write off neither individuals nor Ninevehs. Yet we are to engage in "speaking the truth in love" (Ephesians 4:15), as Joseph Smith did with presidential aspirant Stephen A. Douglas. One wonders if Douglas, in his busy political life, ever paused long enough later in life to let the Holy Ghost preach to him from the pulpit of memory.

Another of the prophet's observations from Liberty Jail, this one to a friendly nonmember, was, "The name Mormon, and Mormonism, was given to us by our enemies, but Latter-day Saints was the real name by which the Church was organized" (*Writings*, p. 420).

Names do matter.

The Good Shepherd taught his followers that his sheep "hear [and know] his voice: and he calleth his own sheep *by name*" (John 10:3–4; italics added). This was how Christ called Peter: "Thou art Simon the son of Jona" (John 1:42).

When the Father and the Son called the leader-prophet of the latter days, Joseph later recorded, "One of them spake unto me, calling me *by name*" (JS—H 1:17; italics added). The pattern of personalization prevailed in Liberty Jail: "Know thou, my son" (D&C 122:7). "Peace be unto thy soul" (D&C 121:7).

As Truman Madsen has observed, the Prophet Joseph's request for a certain hymn to be sung in the final jail was for lyrics that included the line, "He spake, and my poor name he named" ("A Poor Wayfaring Man of Grief," *Hymns* [new edition], no. 29).

This pattern of individualization is not only highly impressive but it also shows individualized love. As the resurrected Jesus prepared to part from his Nephite Twelve, "he spake unto his disciples, *one by one*" asking what they desired of him "after that I am gone to the Father" (3 Nephi 28:1; italics added).

So as we look through the bars at Liberty Jail we see an imperfect but improving Joseph. All was not tidiness or smoothness. Edges and corners were being painfully and obviously knocked off. But Joseph was striving to serve and to become like his perfect Master, Jesus, who had borne so much more—indeed, all! Joseph had "deepness of earth," but it took the harrowing of special experiences to increase his spiritual yield to "a hundred fold" (see Matthew 13:5, 8).

No mortal is to any full degree truly like Jesus. Even so, Jesus had one Judas; Joseph, several. Jesus had one doubting Thomas; Joseph, several. Yet no one was happier than Joseph when prodigals returned, voting with their feet on the road of repentance and reconciliation. Only the meek can finally align intentions and actions.

Near the end of his eventful and revelation-filled ministry, Joseph seemed to realize how difficult it might be for others to understand him fully. "I don't blame any one for not believing my history. If I had not experienced what I have, I would not have believed it myself." (*History of the Church* 6:317.)[1]

Joseph, who lived his life "in crescendo," followed the counsel, "Endure it well." Now it remains for his people to do likewise.

Joseph's sincere words of salutation in a secluded grove ushered in this dispensation. They were words of anxious petition uttered in distress. Joseph said he exerted "all [his] powers to call upon God" (JS—H 1:16).

Twenty-four springs later, Joseph, in a different distress, cried "O Lord my God!" (D&C 135:1.)

God did not fail to respond at either time.

And Joseph Smith did not fail God.

As promised, this "choice seer" lived "to finish the work God had given him to do."

We too must be occupied with our work. Church members today, perhaps more than ever in recent memory, must *first* get their own witness as to the prophetic mission of the Prophet Joseph Smith and *second* be willing to bear that witness publicly and privately. We must not forget the lesson President David O. McKay taught us about how his own discouraged father, while on his mission, was advised by the Spirit that he must declare publicly his testimony of the Prophet Joseph Smith. After he had done this the gloom lifted, and his mission was successful. It will not be otherwise with us today.

The prophecy given by the angel Moroni was that Joseph's name "should be had for good and evil among all nations." The adversary will be doing his relentless part with regard to the negative portion of that prophecy. By word and deed, faithful Church members must see to it that the positive portion is fulfilled.

The latter-day work begun by a latter-day seer is spreading throughout the world. What began when Joseph saw a pillar of glorious light is now a worldwide, burgeoning spiritual light which can no longer be hidden.

No wonder that, with more frequency and in more places, "the ends of the earth . . . inquire after [Joseph's] name"!

Notes

1. Joseph's unusual resilience and his being of good cheer permitted him a special perspective, one full of faith: "And as for the perils which I am called to pass through, they seem but a small thing to me, as the envy and wrath of man have been my common lot all the days of my life. . . . It has all become a second nature to me. . . . I shall triumph over all my enemies, for the Lord God hath spoken it." (D&C 127:2.)

Subject Index

Scripture Index

BOOK OF MORMON